AIRFRAME & POWERPLANT MECHANICS

MECHANICS

AIRFRAME WORKBOOK

FOR USE WITH

FAA-H-8083-31 & FAA-H-8083-31-ATB

Airframe & Powerplant Mechanics Handbook

by Ronald Sterkenburg

Printed and Published by
Aircraft Technical Book Company
72413 US Hwy 40
Tabernash, CO 80478-0270 USA
1 970.726.5111 FAX 1 970.726.5115
www.actechbooks.com

PREFACE

About this Workbook

This Student Workbook is designed as a companion to the Aviation Maintenance Mechanics Airframe Handbook FAA-H-8083-31 and FAA-H-8083-31-ATB. Each chapter of this workbook matches the equivalent chapter in the Handbook and contains study questions, exercises, and a final exam for that chapter. Each is designed to enhance your understanding of the material in the textbook and to better prepare you for success with your actual written exams and later in your career as a professional aviation maintenance technician.

Each chapter of this Workbook is presented in 3 parts:
1] Study Aid Questions are fill in the blank, multiple choice, true or false, and matching formats designed to reinforce the most important concepts presented in the Textbook.
2] Knowledge Application Questions; giving you an opportunity to actually use the material presented in each chapter to solve common problems.
3] Final Chapter Exam, in multiple choice format designed to further reinforce your study skills and to be used by instructors as end of chapter exams and as an evaluation of your progress.

The answers to Sections A & B questions may be found in the back of this workbook and can so be used by students as a part of your personal study habits. The answers to Section C - Final Chapter Exams, are available only to instructors as part of the instructor support package for the H-8083 textbook series, thus preserving the value of the exam as a valid instructional tool.

Each page in this book is perforated allowing students to tear out and turn in assigned sections which may be given as homework or in-class exercises.

For further information about this Workbook, its corresponding Textbook, or to order additional copies in print or electronic format, please contact Aircraft Technical Book Company at 970.726.5111, or email to orders@actechbooks.com, or visit our web site at www.actechbooks.com.

CONTENTS

AIRCRAFT TECHNICAL BOOK COMPANY ...*your professional source*

www.actechbooks.com - The world's largest retailer of books, videos, and software for the aviation technician.

Chapter 1
Aircraft Structures

Chapter 1 - Section A
Study Aid Questions

Fill in the Blanks

1. The part of the aircraft that is designed to carry a load or resist stress is the _____.

2. All aircraft are subjected to five major stresses: tension, compression, bending, _____,

    and _____.

3. Tensile strength is measured in _____ which is written as _____.

4. Wings that require no external bracing are known as _____ design.

5. _____ internal structures are made up of spars and stringers.

6. Spars are to wings as _____ are to the fuselage.

7. I-beam spars are made up of two components: the _____ which is the vertical section and the

    _____ which is the horizontal section.

8. A stainless steel or titanium bulkhead known as a _____ is used to isolate the

    _____ from the rest of the aircraft.

9. Cowl flaps are moveable parts of the cowling that open and close to _____.

10. The primary flight controls include the ailerons, elevators, and rudders which control the stability around the

_____, _____, and _____ axes respectively.

11. Primary flight control surfaces need to be balanced so they do not vibrate or _____.

12. When the aircraft is turned to the left, the aileron on the pilot's _____ points up.

13. Elevators move the aircraft around the _____ axis.

14. When the right pedal is pushed forward, it deflects the rudder to the _____ which moves the nose of the aircraft to the right.

15. Flaps that slide aft to increase the total area of the wing are known as _____ flaps.

16. Slats increase the _____ at which laminar airflow can exist.

17. Heavy or high performance aircraft have _____ on the top of their wings that disrupt airflow when deployed.

18. The _____ is the location from which all other stations are located.

19. Firewalls are typically made from _____.

20. Teetering hinges in a semi-rigid system allow for movement of the flap _____

while preventing movement _____.

TRUE or FALSE

_____ 1. Wing braces are the main structural member of a wing.

_____ 2. Torsion resists pulling forces.

_____ 3. Tensile strength is generally greater than or equal to shearing strength.

_____ 4. Longerons are the longitudinal members in a semimonocoque fuselage.

_____ 5. The benefit of a semimonocoque fuselage compared to a monocoque fuselage is that the semimonocoque fuselage does not require the skin to carry any load thereby reducing the stress on the skin.

_____ 6. Box beam wing constructions are used on transport category aircraft.

_____ 7. False ribs are those ribs which are used strictly for shaping the camber of the wing and do not provide any load support.

_____ 8. Cowlings are detachable panels which provide smooth airflow over the engine and protect it from damage.

_____ 9. Ribs can be lightened by stamping holes in the assembly.

_____ 10. High performance aircraft typically have fly-by-wire systems that utilize electrical power to move the elevators.

_____ 11. Fuel-carrying bladders located in a wing are known as wet wing designs.

_____ 12. Worm drives and flap tracks are used to move fowler flaps along their designed route of travel.

_____ 13. Leading edge flaps are independent of the trailing edge flaps.

_____ 14. Vortex generators are designed to reduce drag created by wingtip vortices.

_____ 15. Conventional gear and tricycle gear are interchangeable terms.

_____ 16. Aircraft equipped with pontoons or floats are sometimes known as amphibious aircraft

_____ 17. Water line measurements are perpendicular to the horizon.

_____ 18. Helicopters are moved horizontally by changing the angle of attack on the rotor blades.

_____ 19. Dissymmetry of lift causes blades to flutter.

_____ 20. Torque produced by the main rotors tries to spin the fuselage in the direction of blade rotation.

1. Why are the rotors of a helicopter considered part of the airframe?

2. Define strain.

3. Describe stresses involved on a part being bent or subject to bending stress.

4. Cowlings and fairings do not require a high degree of strength but what characteristic is important for parts such as these?

5. What are the structural members that make up a truss-framed fuselage and what is it typically covered with?

6. What is the biggest problem associated with the monocoque type fuselage?

7. How is the monocoque type fuselage different than the semi-monocoque type?

8. What causes metal fatigue in a pressurized aircraft fuselage structure?

9. When is the use of landing gear jury struts necessary and what purpose do they serve?

10. What is the function of the wing spar?

11. Where are false ribs located and what is their function?

12. Describe the characteristics of a nacelle and its components.

13. Directional control of a fixed-wing aircraft takes place around which axes? What are the respective control surfaces that move about these axes?

14. What affect does moving the aileron down have on the wing?

15. What are the functions of slots and where are they located?

16. How are balance tabs moved and what is their resulting effect?

17. What is the main benefit of conventional type landing gear?

18. Why are ground loops common on conventional landing gear?

19. Describe the cause(s) of dissymmetry of lift.

20. What is the NOTAR antitorque system and how does it work?

name: _____

Chapter 1 - Section C
Final Chapter Exam

1. The study that calculates the loads that every part of an aircraft must carry is known as
    a. Stress analysis
    b. Tension analysis
    c. Load testing

2. The material's internal resistance or counterforce that opposes deformation is called
    a. Rigidity
    b. Strength
    c. Stress

3. What type of stress resists a crushing force?
    a. Tension
    b. Compression
    c. Torsion

4. What type of stress is a combination of compression and tension?
    a. Torsion
    b. Shear
    c. Bending

5. What type of construction method is used for most aluminum aircraft constructions?
    a. Monocoque
    b. Semimonocoque
    c. Truss

6. What is the angle called that is made between the fuselage and the horizontal plane of the wing?
    a. Angle of attack
    b. Wing dihedral
    c. Angle of incidence

7. What is the principle structural member of the wing?
    a. Spars
    b. Ribs
    c. Stringers

8. How is the load transferred from the skin and the stringers to the spars?
    a. Stiffeners
    b. Caps
    c. Ribs

9. Where are wing butt ribs located?
    a. Forward of the front spar
    b. In between the front and rear spar
    c. At the inboard edge of the wing

10. What is the purpose of a fairing?
    a. Allows for smooth airflow between the wing and fuselage
    b. Provide a strong and secure method for attaching the wing to the fuselage
    c. Receives compression loads that tend to force the wing spars together

11. What are the names of the movable flight control surfaces on the empennage?
    a. Horizontal stabilizer and elevator
    b. Vertical stabilizer and rudder
    c. Elevator and rudder

12. What flight control surface movement causes the aircraft to roll?
    a. Aileron
    b. Elevator
    c. Rudder

13. What type of movement does the rudder control?
    a. Roll
    b. Pitch
    c. Yaw

14. What is a common design feature of ailerons to prevent flutter?
    a. Hinge points aft of the leading edge
    b. Hinge points forward of the leading edge
    c. Hinge points at the leading edge

15. As the aileron moves downward, what happens to the camber and lift respectively?
    a. Camber increases, lift decreases
    b. Camber decreases, lift decreases
    c. Camber increases, lift increases

16. How is the elevator controlled from the cockpit?
    a. Side-to-side motion of the control yoke
    b. Push and pull motion of the control yoke
    c. Depressing of foot-operated pedals

17. Which two types of control surfaces reduce the force needed to move a primary control surface?
    a. Anti-balance and servo tabs
    b. Trim and balance tabs
    c. Slats and spoilers

18. What type of secondary flight control decreases lift?
    a. Slats
    b. Slots
    c. Spoilers

19. Which control surface can be operated independently of the flaps?
    a. Leading edge flaps
    b. Slats
    c. Neither A or B

20. Spoilers may be fully deployed on both wings at the same time for what purpose?
    a. Augment aileron function
    b. Decrease lift in-flight
    c. Speed brakes

21. What flight control tabs move in same direction as the control surface it is attached to?
    a. Trim
    b. Spring
    c. Anti-balance

22. How are flight control surfaces moved on an aircraft that is equipped with a fly-by-wire system?
    a. Electrical input only
    b. Hydraulic actuators and electrical input
    c. Control cables only

23. What type of device is used as a barrier on the upper surface of the wing to reduce the tendency of the wing to stall at low flight speeds?
    a. Stall fence
    b. Vortex generator
    c. Gap seals

24. Where is the center of gravity located on an aircraft with a tricycle landing gear?
    a. Forward of the main wheels
    b. Aft of the main wheels
    c. In-line with the main wheels

25. Fuselage stations are numbered in inches from _____
    a. The buttock line
    b. Reference datum
    c. Water line

26. _____ is a measurement forward or aft of the front spar and perpendicular to the water line.
    a. Aileron station
    b. Flap station
    c. Nacelle station

27. Where can one find information on panel numbering and the location of components under each panel?
    a. AC 43.13
    b. TCDS
    c. Maintenance manual

28. How are main rotors of helicopters classified?
    a. The transmission used to power the rotors
    b. Blade attachment and motion relative to the hub
    c. Swash plate and pitch change units attached to the blade

29. How is the pitch of the rotor blades changed in a rigid rotor system?
    a. Feathering hinges
    b. Coning hinges
    c. Teetering hinges

30. What is the windspeed and lift developed by the advancing blade in relation to the retreating blade?
    a. Greater windspeed, less lift
    b. Slower windspeed, less lift
    c. Greater windspeed, more lift

Chapter 2 - Aerodynamics, Assembly, & Rigging

Chapter 2 - Section A
Study Aid Questions

Fill in the Blanks

1. The study of objects in motion through the air and the _____ governing that

   motion come from the Greek combination of "aero" and "_____".

2. Atmospheric pressure is measured in _____ with a _____.

3. As an aircraft descends atmospheric pressure _____, the amount of oxygen in the air

   _____, and temperature _____.

4. Density varies _____ with temperature and _____ with pressure.

5. A body at rest does not move unless a force is applied to it is Newton's _____ law and is

   known as the law of _____.

6. According to Bernoulli's principle, fluid flowing through a constriction experiences a(n) _____
   in speed.

7. Velocity increases and pressure decreases on the _____ of the wing.

8. A pilot can increase the lift of an aircraft by increasing the _____.

9. The acute angle the wing chord makes with the _____ axis is called angle of incidence.

10. The boundary layer is the layer of _____ closest to the surface and its behavior

    is controlled in order to minimize _____ drag and skin friction drag.

11. Fluids always move from _____ to _____ pressure. This principle explains

    the spanwise movement of air flow from the bottom of the wing _____ and upward

    around the wing creating spillage over the wingtip called _____.

12. An object that tends to returns to equilibrium is said to have positive _____ stability.

13. _____ control the lateral movements of the aircraft, the _____

    controls the longitudinal movements, and the _____ controls the directional movements.

14. An autogryo is an aircraft with a horizontal rotor that is _____ and turns due to the

    passage of air _____ through the rotor.

15. The blade with the decreased angle of attack tends to flap_____.

16. The collective pitch control is operated with the _____ hand and is used to make pitch angle

    changes to _____ the main rotor blades.

17. There is a _____ of lift between the advancing and retreating blade.

18. Autorotation is possible through a freewheeling unit, a special _____ mechanism, which
    automatically disengages the engine in the event of its failure.

19. Helicopters with tandem rotors use the pedals to tilt the main rotors. When the _____ pedal

    is pushed forward the aft rotor moves to the _____.

20. Swaging tools generally have a _____ dimensions in an attempt to avoid defective or inferior swages.

21. Cables that travel completely through bulkheads require the use of a _____ and should not be deflected more than _____ from a straight line.

22. A groove or knurl around the end of the barrel of a _____ can be used to identify the _____ threads.

23. Structural alignment is the _____ of the main structural component related to the longitudinal datum line parallel to the aircraft centerline and the lateral datum line parallel to the line joining the _____.

24. Hard landings and abnormal flight experiences prompt a check of the wing _____ and angle of _____.

25. The most common method of safety wiring is the _____ however; a _____ method can be used for smaller screws and tight spaces.

TRUE or FALSE

_____ 1. Air is considered a fluid.

_____ 2. Atmospheric pressure changes with altitude.

_____ 3. Aircraft can fly faster at lower altitudes because there is more pulling force from the engine cutting through the air

_____ 4. Density varies directly with humidity.

_____ 5. Airflow over an airfoil can be explained using Bernoulli's principle and this pressure differential is called lift.

_____ 6. One wing can have numerous airfoil sections each with unique properties.

_____ 7. The efficiency of a wing is measured in terms of wing camber and AOA.

_____ 8. An aircraft has four forces acting upon it at all times: gravity, lift, thrust and weight.

_____ 9. Induced drag increases as AOA increase.

_____ 10. Center of pressure has the greatest affect on the stability of an aircraft.

_____ 11. The vertical stabilizer is the primary surface that controls directional stability on the horizontal axis.

_____ 12. Trim tabs enable the pilot to correct any unbalanced condition that may exist during flight without touching the flight controls.

_____ 13. Canards are often used in swept wing aircraft to prevent spanwise air movements at high angles of attack.

_____ 14. Stick shakers were installed in hydromechanical flight control systems which provide an artificial stall warning.

_____ 15. At high forward speed a situation called retreating blade stall can occur because of the high AOA and slow relative wind speed.

_____ 16. Control surfaces must be rebalanced whenever there is weight added to a control surface.

_____ 17. The balance beam rebalancing method requires a specialized manufacturer made tool.

_____ 18. Lead and steel are the most common materials used to balance control surfaces.

_____ 19. The Type certification Data Sheet is issued by the manufacturer and includes information such as airspeed limitations, weight limits, and fuel type.

_____ 20. A 7x19 cable is very rigid and used for engine controls and trim tab controls.

_____ 21. Soldering cable ends is a common technique used to prevent fraying.

_____ 22. Cables are checked for corrosion by bending them.

_____ 23. A double-wrap safety wire method is preferred when securing a turnbuckle.

_____ 24. Rudder alignment is done by removing the controls surface from its hinges and passing a plumb bob though the hinge attachment holes.

_____ 25. Cotter pins, unlike safety wire, can be re-used.

name: _____

Chapter 2 - Section B
Knowledge Application Questions

1. Why is air considered a fluid?

2. What is atmospheric pressure and how is it measured?

3. What is the relationship between density, pressure, and temperature?

4. What is the difference between absolute humidity and relative humidity?

5. What is Newton's third law and what does it state?

6. Describe how Bernoulli's principle relates to a wing.

10. Which of the following type of aircraft structures reduce fuel consumption and increases range?
    a. Wing fences
    b. Winglets
    c. Both A & B

11. Compressible aerodynamics deals with speeds at
    a. Mach I and above
    b. 250 mph and below
    c. Mach 3-Mach 5

12. Supersonic flight refers to flight between
    a. 0-Mach 1
    b. Mach 1-Mach 3
    c. Mach 5 and above

13. What type of rotor is found on aircraft with dual rotor blades?
    a. Fully articulated
    b. Semi rigid
    c. Rigid

14. Drift in the direction of the tail rotor during hover is called
    a. Ground effect
    b. Translational tendency
    c. Translational lift

15. Effective translational lift is experienced at what airspeed?
    a. Between hover and 16 knots
    b. Between 16-24 knots
    c. 24 knots and above

16. A helicopter with counterclockwise rotating main rotor would experience which of the following conditions if dissymmetry of lift were allowed to exist with no corrective action?
    a. Roll to the left
    b. Roll to the right
    c. Drift to the left

17. How does a pilot compensate for blowback?
    a. Move the cyclic forward
    b. Move the cyclic aft
    c. Pull up on the collective

18. What component transmits the control inputs from the collective and cyclic to the main rotor blades?
    a. Transmission
    b. Control rod
    c. Swash plate

19. Where is the throttle control located in a helicopter?
    a. On the collective
    b. On the cyclic
    c. On a lever next to the collective

20. What is the primary purpose of the helicopter main rotor transmission?
    a. Increase engine output RPM to optimum rotor RPM
    b. Decrease engine output RPM to optimum rotor RPM
    c. Synchronize the rotation of the engine with the rotor

21. During static balancing, an upward movement of the trailing edge of a control surface on a balance stand indicates:
    a. An overbalance designated with a (+) sign
    b. An underbalance designated with a (-) sign
    c. An overbalance designated with a (-) sign

22. Which rebalancing method can be performed without removing the control surface from the aircraft?
    a. Calculation method
    b. Scale method
    c. Balance beam method

23. Where should rigging and alignment checks be performed?
    a. On the ramp
    b. In an enclosed hangar
    c. At a specialized maintenance facility

24. _____ may be used to force the primary nut thread against the bolt or screw thread.
    a. Lock nut
    b. Lock washer
    c. Pal nut

25. ELT tests should be conducted
    a. During the last 5 minutes of any hour
    b. During the first 5 minutes of any hour
    c. During the first 15 minutes of any hour

Chapter 3 - Fabric Covering

Chapter 3 - Section A
Study Aid Questions

Fill in the Blanks

1. Organic fabrics, like linen and _____, were the original fabrics used for covering airframes but

   their tendency to _____ gave way to a process known as _____.

2. Organic fabrics generally only last _____ years.

3. _____ fabric is the standard covering currently being used in the United States.

4. Pinked edges have been cut into a continuous series of V's by machine or special _____

   to prevent _____.

5. Deviations from the supplemental type certificate in any way renders the aircraft _____.

6. A _____ field approval may be acquired to deviate from the original covering process or material.

7. _____ is the single most destructive element that causes polyester fabric to deteriorate.

8. To achieve a level and deep glossy finish, _____ is added to slow dry time.

9. Finishing tape is used to cover all _____ and rib lacing to provide a smooth finish and

   _____.

10. Fungicide and mildewicide are only required for _____ fabric.

11. Loose fabric affects the _____ distribution and _____ the airframe.

12. A _____ may be used per the manufacturer's instruction if the dope coating is found to have cracks but the fabric itself is still _____.

13. Breaking strength is determined by cutting a test strip, taken from an area that is _____ to the elements, which is _____ by 4-6 inches.

14. The _____ method of re-covering uses multiple flat sections of fabric attached to the frame whereas the envelope method uses _____ envelopes to cover the aircraft.

15. It is important in the re-covering process that the _____, _____, and ventilation be controlled.

16. Fabric coatings should be applied with a high-_____, low-_____ sprayer.

17. Some of the primary concerns of fabric seams are strength, elasticity, _____ and good _____.

18. Closer spacing of rib lacing should be done in the area that experiences _____, about one propeller width plus _____.

19. Inspection rings are left intact and only removed when _____ is required. It is then closed using preformed _____ panels.

20. Fabric gussets, installed as _____, reinforce cable guide openings and _____-attached fitting areas.

TRUE or FALSE

_____ 1. Warp describes the direction across the width of the fabric.

_____ 2. The same materials and techniques must be used when replacing aircraft fabric.

_____ 3. A TSO is a technical standard order issued by the manufacturer for specific parts, materials, processes, and appliances use on civil aircraft.

_____ 4. Only companies with a PMA may manufacture and sell aviation fabric.

_____ 5. The same thread may be used to hand sew and machine sew aviation fabric.

_____ 6. Prior to airframe covering, the structure must be primed.

_____ 7. Fabric cement is used to attach the fabric to the airframe.

_____ 8. Fabric is still airworthy down to 70% of the breaking strength of new fabric.

_____ 9. Fabric test strips should have all the coatings left on to get an accurate measurement of the fabric's breaking strength.

_____ 10. Punch testers like Seyboth and Maule give an accurate representation of the fabric breaking strength.

_____ 11. The Maule punch tester does not puncture airworthy fabric during testing.

_____ 12. Fuselage and wings can be covered with one large envelope.

_____ 13. Many of the substances used to re-cover an aircraft are highly toxic.

_____ 14. Old adhesive stuck to the airframe can be removed with MEK.

_____ 15. Polyester fabric generally incorporates sewn seams.

_____ 16. An ordinary household iron may be used to heat shrink fabric.

_____ 17. Heat shrinking should be done evenly by starting from one end and progressing to the other end.

_____ 18. Finishing tape is applied to all seams, edges, and ribs.

_____ 19. Wing leading edges usually receive the narrowest amount of finishing tape to reduce irregularities during the covering process.

_____ 20. There is no compromise in strength between cemented repairs and sewn repairs.

name: _____

1. How do aircraft designers address the flammability of nitrate doping and the process they used for application?

2. Explain why replacing cotton fabric with polyester fabric aircraft is considered a major alteration.

3. Describe what anti-chafe tape is and when it is used.

4. Describe the difference between hand thread and machine thread.

5. How are the holes inside grommets created?

6. Explain the process of re-covering an aircraft using the blanket method.

7. What are some of the necessary personal protection equipment needed when re-covering an aircraft?

8. What is used to produce a smooth finish on leading edges of aluminum wings? What is essential when considering this process?

9. Describe the process of heat shrinking fabric.

10. What is the purpose of a drain grommet and where are they located?

11. How are finishing tapes applied at the leading and trailing edges?

12. What is fabric primer and what does it do?

1. What does the term bias mean in relation to fabric coverings?
    a. The weave across the width of the fabric
    b. The warp along the direction of the fabric
    c. A cut or fold made at a diagonal to the warp

2. Which 14 CFR part 43 Appendix states what maintenance actions are considered minor and major repairs?
    a. A
    b. B
    c. C

3. Major fabric repairs need to be inspected by?
    a. Airframe mechanic
    b. Airframe and Powerplant mechanic
    c. Airframe and Powerplant mechanic with an Inspection Authorization

4. Where is reinforcing tape most commonly used?
    a. Seams
    b. Rib caps
    c. Around inspection rings

5. Which of the following is used to create reinforced drain holes in aircraft fabric?
    a. Inspection rings
    b. Spring clips
    c. Grommets

6. What type of coating is applied to protect the fabric from UV light?
    a. Primer
    b. Sealer
    c. Filler

7. When is accelerator used when applying fabric topcoats?
    a. Temperatures below ideal working temperatures
    b. Temperatures above ideal working temperatures
    c. Humidity above ideal working conditions

8. What is the key ingredient in the Poly-Fiber covering system?
    a. Polyurethane
    b. Vinyl
    c. Water-based glue

9. Aircraft with wing loading of 9 lb/ft^2 and over should have fabric strength at or above:
    a. Grade A
    b. Intermediate grade
    c. Lightweight

10. Aircraft with a V_{NE} of 135 mph or less are considered to be unairworthy when the fabric breaking strength has deteriorated to below:
    a. 56
    b. 46
    c. 35

11. Re-covering a fabric aircraft is considered:
    a. A minor repair or alteration
    b. A major repair or alteration
    c. General maintenance

12. Which fabric covering system is nonhazardous?
    a. Superflite
    b. Air-Tech
    c. Stewart

13. Critical airflow areas such as the leading edge require how many inches of overlap at the seam?
    a. 1-2
    b. 2-4
    c. 4-6

14. How much does polyester fabric shrink at 350°F?
    a. 5%
    b. 8%
    c. 10%

15. Which of the following repairs require sewing?
    a. Cotton fabric repairs
    b. Polyester fabric repairs
    c. Neither A or B

16. Where can technicians find instructions about tying the correct knots during the rib lacing process?
    a. STC and maintenance manuals
    b. AC 43.13-1
    c. Both A & B

17. What should be applied to rib caps that are not rounded over?
    a. Anti-chafe tape
    b. Reinforcing tape
    c. Surface tape

18. How many blankets does it usually take to cover a wing?
    a. 1
    b. 2
    c. At least 4

19. Which of the following is not a FAA approved method of testing?
    a. Test strip method
    b. IA visual and NDT inspection method
    c. Mechanical fabric strength testers

20. Which of the following fabrics is no longer available?
    a. Grade A cotton
    b. Lightweight polyester
    c. Ceconite 101

21. Which tape is already pre-shrunk?
    a. Anti-chafe tape
    b. Rib bracing tape
    c. Surface tape

22. What additive increases the overall flexibility and life of a coating?
    a. Thinner
    b. Retarder
    c. Rejuvenator

23. Finishing tape (surface tape) is used for what purpose?
    a. To help prevent 'ripple formation' in covering fabric.
    b. To provide additional anti-tear resistance under reinforcement tape.
    c. To provide additional wear resistance over the edges of fabric forming structures.

24. The determining factor(s) for the selection of the correct weight of textile fabric to be used in covering any type of aircraft is the
    a. maximum wing loading.
    b. speed of the aircraft.
    c. speed of the aircraft and the maximum wing loading.

25. Any protrusions in the fabric covering are reinforced with:
    a. Rings
    b. Grommets
    c. Gussets

Chapter 4 - Aircraft Metal

Chapter 4 - Section A
Study Aid Questions

Fill in the Blanks

1. A joint that is too weak cannot be tolerated, but neither can one that is too _____ because

   it can create stress risers that may cause _____ in other locations.

2. There are six types of stresses: tension, compression, _____, and bearing are known as

   basic stresses; while bending and _____ (or twisting) are considered combination stresses.

3. There are two ways to determine rivet size: (1) the size of rivets in the next _____ rivet row

   inboard on the wing and (2) multiple the thickness of the thickest sheet by _____ and
   use the next larger size.

4. Aircraft structural joint design involves an attempt to find the optimum strength relationship between being

   critical in _____ and critical in _____.

5. A file with a single row of _____ teeth is called a single-cut file; whereas files with one row

   of teeth crossing under another row are called _____ files.

6. Files are classified according to their _____. The most common files include: flat, triangle,

   square, _____, and round.

7. _____ drill motors are recommended for use on projects around flammable materials

   where potentials spark from a(n) _____ drill motor might become a fire hazard.

8. Properly adjusted drill _____ can prevent excessive drill penetration that might damage the

   _____ structure or injure personnel.

9. A bar folder is designed for use in making _____ or folds along edges of sheet metal.

10. _____ breaks are used to form thicker more _____ parts.

11. On the slip roll, the front rollers _____ or grip the metal sheet while the rear

    roll provides the proper _____ to the work.

12. It is advantageous to _____ or even polish the edges of a flange that must undergo

    even moderate _____ to avoid crack formation.

13. _____ made of hardwood are widely used in airframe metalwork for shrinking and

    stretching metal, particularly angles and _____.

14. The minimum bend radius is affected by; the kind of material, _____ of the material, and

    _____ condition of the material.

15. The _____ must be used for all bend that are smaller or larger than _____.

16. In order to form a box, it is necessary to drill _____ at the intersection of the inside

    bend _____ lines.

17. Machining characteristics of magnesium are _____, making possible the use of maximum

    speeds of the machine tools with heavy cuts and high _____ rates.

18. Rivets fill the hole during the installation process which provides a good _____ transfer.

19. Blind rivets are installed during _____ where access is not available to form the

    driven head of _____ rivets.

20. The CherryMax rivet consists of five parts; _____ blind header, hollow rivet shell,

    _____ collar, driving anvil, and the pulling stem.

21. Collars used with Hi-Lok fasteners have a _____ break-off groove which shears off at a

    predetermined _____, leaving the lower portion of the collar seated with the proper torque.

22. An interference fit is typically used for _____ and _____ fit
    is used for steel, titanium, and composites.

23. Rivnuts are internally threaded _____ that have a flush or shallow _____
    heads.

24. Rivet diameter should not be _____ than 3 times the thickness of the _____ sheet.

25. Rivet _____ is the distance between the centers of _____ rivets
    in the same row.

26. If countersinking is done on metal below a certain thickness a _____ with less than

    minimum bearing surface or _____ of the hole may occur.

27. A rivet gun with the correct header must be held snugly against the head and _____

    to the surface while the bucking bar of the proper _____ is held against the opposite end.

28. _____ repair is very important because of the load it carries and particular care should

    be taken to ensure the original _____ of the structure is not impaired.

29. A scale or _____ can be used to check the condition of the upset rivet head to see that it conforms to the proper requirements.

30. _____ dimpling is the process that uses heated dimpling dies so that the material will

_____ better during the dimpling process.

1 - Matching   (answers may be used more than once)

a. Tension	c. Shear	e. Torsion
b. Compression	d. Bearing	f. Bending

_____ 1. The force that resists the force that rivets or bolts place on a hole.

_____ 2. The force per unit area which causes adjacent particles of material to slide past each other.

_____ 3. A combination of two forces acting upon a structural member at one or more points.

_____ 4. The force which tends to twist a structural member.

_____ 5. The force per unit area which tends to stretch a structural member.

_____ 6. The force per unit area which tends to shorten a structural member at any cross section.

_____ 7.

_____ 10.

_____ 8.

_____ 11.

_____ 9.

2 - Matching

a. Brinelling	b. Burnishing	c. Burr	d. Corrosion	e. Crack	f. Cut
g. Dent	h. Erosion	i. Chattering	j. Galling	k. Gouge	l. Inclusion
m. Nick	n. Pitting	o. Scratch	p. Score	q. Stain	r. Upsetting

_____ 1. Presence of foreign or extraneous material wholly within a portion of metal

_____ 2. A small, thin section of metal extending beyond a regular surface

_____ 3. Breakdown or deterioration of metal surface by vibratory action

_____ 4. A change in color, locally causing a noticeably different appearance

_____ 5. Loss of metal, usually to an appreciable depth over a relatively long, narrow area

_____ 6. Occurrence of shallow, spherical depressions in a surface

_____ 7. A physical separation of two adjacent portions of metal

_____ 8. Slight tear or break in metal surface from light contact by a foreign object

_____ 9. Indentation in a metal surface produced by an object striking with force

_____ 10. Loss of metal from the surface by chemical or electrochemical action

_____ 11. Deep tear or break in metal surface from contact under pressure

_____ 12. Breakdown of metal surfaces due to excessive friction between two part

_____ 13. Local break or notch on edge

_____ 14. A displacement of material beyond the normal contour or surface

_____ 15. Polishing of one surface by sliding contact with a smooth, hard surface

_____ 16. Loss of metal from the surface by mechanical action of foreign object

_____ 17. Sharp, localized breakdown of metal surface with defined edges

_____ 18. Grooves in a metal surface from contact with foreign material under heavy pressure

3 - Matching

a. scales	b. combination square	c. dividers
d. rivet spacer	e. marking tool	f. scribes
g. punches	h. awls	i. hole duplicator

_____ 1. Makes quick and accurate rivet pattern lay-outs on a sheet

_____ 2. Only used when marks will be removed by drilling or cutting

_____ 3. A scale with three heads that can be moved to any position on the scale

_____ 4. A carbon steel tempered marking tool

_____ 5. Comes in lengths most commonly 6" and 12"

_____ 6. Used to locate and match existing holes in structures

_____ 7. Fiber tipped pen

_____ 8. Used in aircraft maintenance to align holes

_____ 9. Transfer measurement from a device to a scale to determine its value

4 - Matching

a. prick punch	b. center punch	c. automatic center punch	
d. transfer punch	e. pin punch	f. drive punch	g. chassis punch

_____ 1. Has an adjustable cap for regulating the stroke

_____ 2. Used to transfer dimensions from a paper pattern directly onto metal

_____ 3. Also known as a drift punch

_____ 4. Used to mark the locations of new holes using a template or existing holes

_____ 5. Used to make holes in sheet metal

_____ 6. Used to make large indentations in metal for a twist drill

_____ 7. Used to drive out damaged rivets, pins and bolts

5 - Matching

_____ 1. Body

_____ 3. Cutting Lips

_____ 5. Flute

_____ 2. Land

_____ 4. Notched Point Chisel Edges

_____ 6. Shank

6 - Matching

a. leg	b. flange	c. grain of metal	d. bend radius
e. neutral axis	f. mold line	g. mold point	h. bend tangent line
i. setback	j. flat	k. bend allowance	l. bend line
m. closed angle	n. open angle	o. K factor	p. total developed

_____ 1. Located where the metal starts to bend and the metal stops curving

_____ 2. Set even with the nose of the brake and acts as a guide for bending

_____ 3. Measured from a radius center to the inside surface of the metal

_____ 4. Width of material, measured around the bends from edge to edge

_____ 5. The distance from the mold point to the bend tangent line

_____ 6. angle that is more than 90° when measured between legs

_____ 7. Line formed by extending the outside surface of the leg and flange to a point in space

_____ 8. The longer part of a formed angle

_____ 9. The curved section of metal within the bend

_____ 10. The shorter part of a formed angle

_____ 11. Corresponds to one of the angles to which metal can be bent

_____ 12. An imaginary line that has the same length after bending as it had before

_____ 13. The base measurement minus setback (=MLD-SB)

_____ 14. The point of intersection of the mold lines

_____ 15. Angle that is more than 90° when the amount of bend is measured

_____ 16. Bend should preferably be made to lie at an angle to this width

7 - Matching

| a. universal head | c. standard 100° flush head | e. modified 120° countersink |
| b. modified universal head | d. reduced flush head | f. cherry hollow end E-Z buck |

_____ 1. Designed specifically for double-flush applications

_____ 2. Are not to be used where aerodynamics is a factor

_____ 3. Designed to limit rivet tipping

_____ 4. Replacement for both round and brazier head rivets

_____ 5. Sacrifice clamp-up strength for increased shear strength

_____ 6. Ideal for dimpling

_____ 7.

_____ 8.

_____ 9.

_____ 10.

8 - Matching

a. 1100 Aluminum   c. 2117 Aluminum   e. 2024 Aluminum   g. Monel
b. 5056 Aluminum   d. 2017 Aluminum   f. 7050 Aluminum

_____ 1.

_____ 2.

_____ 3.

_____ 4. (raised dot)

_____ 5.

_____ 6. (dimple)

_____ 7.

_____ 8. Alloy code-E

_____ 9. Alloy code-AD

_____ 10. Alloy code-M

_____ 11. Alloy code-DD

_____ 12. Alloy code-B

_____ 13. Alloy code-A

9 - Fill in the Box

Fill In the Blank
Minimum Edge Distance

Edge distance/edge margin	Minimum edge distance	Preferred edge distance
Protruding head rivets	1.	2.
Countersunk rivets	3.	4.

10 - Fill in the Box

Rivet pitch/spacing

Rivet spacing	Minimum spacing	Preferred spacing
1 and 3 rows protruding head rivet layout	1.	2.
2 row protruding head rivet lay out	3.	4.
1 and 3 rows countersunk head rivet layout	5.	6.
2 row countersunk head rivet lay out	7.	8.

name: _____

1. Repairs must accomplish which of the following?
    a. accept stresses, carry them across the repair, and dissipate them in the appropriate area
    b. accept stresses, carry them across the repair, and transfer them back to the original structure
    c. accept stresses and disperse them throughout the repair
    d. accept stresses and prevent a continuous path for stresses to build

2. What is needed when control surface repairs alter the weight distribution?
    a. trim tabs are adjusted
    b. counter-balance weight is added
    c. balance weights are removed or added
    d. balancing patches are used

3. What must be done after holes are drilled in aluminum sheet metal?
    a. reamed
    b. deburred
    c. sanded
    d. brushed

4. Lubricants do all of the following except
    a. assist in chip removal
    b. prolongs drill life
    c. prevents overheating
    d. assists in dimensional accuracy of the hole

5. Straight line forming machines include all of the following except
    a. bar folder
    b. cornice break
    c. combination break
    d. box and pan break

6. What is needed for the press break to bend narrow U-channels?
    a. gooseneck dies
    b. offset dies
    c. both A & B
    d. the press break cannot bend narrow U-channels

7. What objects can a box and pan break form that a cornice break cannot?
    a. box
    b. bowl
    c. narrow U-channel
    d. hat channel stringers

8. What is an excellent technique for avoiding stresses at the edge of a part?
    a. use shims to avoid direct clamping on the part
    b. deburring the edges of the part before bending
    c. use mild steel instead of annealed aluminum
    d. both A & B

9. What is used to support the bumping process?
   a. anvil
   b. sandbag
   c. dies
   d. dollies

10. Which of the following is not a factor to consider when forming straight bends?
    a. thickness of the material
    b. alloy composition
    c. setback
    d. temper condition

11. For calculation purposes, where is the neutral axis located in terms of thickness?
    a. .5T
    b. .445T
    c. .545T

12. (refer to table below) What is the minimum bend radius of a .063" thick piece of 6061-T6 aluminum alloy?
    a. .16
    b. .12
    c. .44
    d. .03

CHART 204
MINIMUM BEND RADIUS FOR ALUMINUM ALLOYS

THICKNESS	5052-0 6061-0 5052-H32	7178-0 2024-0 5052-H34 6061-T4 7075-0	6061-T6	7075-T6	2024-T3 2024-T4	2024-T6
.012	.03	.03	.03	.03	.06	.06
.016	.03	.03	.03	.03	.09	.09
.020	.03	.03	.03	.12	.09	.09
.025	.03	.03	.06	.16	.12	.09
.032	.03	.03	.06	.19	.12	.12
.040	.06	.06	.09	.22	.16	.16
.050	.06	.06	.12	.25	.19	.19
.063	.06	.09	.16	.31	.22	.25
.071	.09	.12	.16	.38	.25	.31
.080	.09	.16	.19	.44	.31	.38
.090	.09	.19	.22	.50	.38	.44
.100	.12	.22	.25	.62	.44	.50
.125	.12	.25	.31	.88	.50	.62
.160	.16	.31	.44	1.25	.75	.75
.190	.19	.38	.56	1.38	1.00	1.00
.250	.31	.62	.75	2.00	1.25	1.25
.312	.44	1.25	1.38	2.50	1.50	1.50
.375	.44	1.38	1.50	2.50	1.88	1.88

BEND RADIUS IS DESIGNATED TO THE INSIDE OF THE BEND.
ALL DIMENSIONS ARE IN INCHES.

13. What is the formula to calculate bend allowance?

   a. $BA= \dfrac{2(R+1/2T)}{4\Pi}$

   b. $BA= \dfrac{2(R+1/2T)}{4}$

   c. $BA= \dfrac{2\Pi(R+1/2T)}{4}$

14. How large are relief holes used in forming boxes?
    a. 2 times the thickness of the material
    b. 2 time the bend radius
    c. 2 times the bend angle

15. The distance between the two bends of a joggle is called the
    a. neutral axis
    b. allowance
    c. J- intersection

16. What can be done to prevent cracking in the bend area when bending CRES?
    a. use a bend radius smaller than recommended in the minimum bend radius table
    b. use a bend radius larger than recommended in the minimum bend radius table
    c. heat the CRES before bending

17. What rivets are used for joining corrosion resistant steel and titanium parts together?
    a. 7050 Aluminum
    b. 5056 Aluminum
    c. Monel

18. CherryMax rivets are manufactured with all of the following head styles except:
    a. universal
    b. unisink
    c. 120° flush head
    d. 130° countersunk

19. All of the following are advantages of Hi-lok fasteners except:
    a. light weight
    b. high fatigue resistant
    c. high heat tolerance
    d. high strength

20. Which of the following is a permanent type fastener assembly that consists of a pin and collar?
    a. lockbolt
    b. CherryBUCK
    c. Taper-lok
    d. Eddie-bolt

21. Correct rivet installation requires all of the following except:
    a. dimpling of the skin
    b. good hole preparations
    c. removal of burrs
    d. clamping the sheets together

22. Transverse pitch is the perpendicular distance between rivet rows and is usually equal to
    a. 50% of the rivet pitch
    b. 75% of the rivet pitch
    c. 90% of the rivet pitch

23. When using a rivet size of 1/8", what drill size should be used?
    a. #40
    b. #30
    c. #21

24. Which of the following is not a common type of countersunk wells?
    a. 82°
    b. 120°
    c. 110°

25. The NACA riveting method has primary applications in
    a. leading edge areas
    b. trailing edge areas
    c. fuel tank areas

26. What should you be looking for when inspecting rivets?
    a. paint chipped off rivet heads
    b. smoking or working rivets (black ring around rivet)
    c. skin bulging around the rivet
    d. all of the above

27. Fuselage stringers extend from the
    a. nose to the tail
    b. leading edge to the trailing edge
    c. wingtip to wingtip

28. The spar is the main supporting member of the
    a. fuselage
    b. empennage
    c. wing

29. What is the purpose of refrigerating 2017 and 2024 aluminum alloy rivets after heat treatment?
    a. to accelerate age hardening
    b. to relieve internal stresses
    c. to retard age hardening

30. The dimensions of an MS20470AD-4-8 rivet are
    a. 1/8 inch in diameter and ¼ inch long
    b. 1/8 inch in diameter and ½ inch long
    c. 4/16 inch in diameter and 8/32 inch long

Chapter 5 - Aircraft Welding

Chapter 5 - Section A
Study Aid Questions

Fill in the Blanks

1. There are 3 types of welding: _____, _____ and, _____ welding.

2. The oxy acetylene flame, with a temperature of _____ Fahrenheit is produced with a torch burning _____ and mixing it with _____.

3. Shielded metal arc welding is the most common type and often referred to as _____ welding.

4. Gas metal arc welding (GMAW) was formerly called _____.

5. When welding mild steel, stainless steel, or titanium the welder setting needs to be set to _____ _____ . When welding aluminum and magnesium _____ must be selected.

6. Electric resistance welding, either _____ or _____ welding is typically used to join thin sheet metal components.

7. The gas used with Plasma Arc Welding is _____. The torch also uses secondary gas such as _____ or _____ that assists in shielding the puddle.

8. Argon is _____, _____, _____ and nontoxic.

9. The oxygen hose is _____ and has _____ threads indicated by the absence of a groove.

10. The size of the tip opening not _____ determines how much heat is applied to the work.

11. All cylinders should be stored and transported in the _____ position, especially

    acetylene because they contain an absorbent material saturated with _____

12. The higher the welding tip number the _____ the hole in the tip.

13. Three flame types flame commonly used for welding are _____,

    _____, and _____.

14. The oxidizing flame burns at approximately _____°F and is produced by burning an excess

    of _____.

15. A _____ may be caused by touching the tip to the work, _____

    the tip, by a _____ tip, or by dirt or slag in the end of the tip.

16. Turn off the flame by closing the _____ valve on the torch first. Then close the

    _____ valve on the torch.

17. Low _____, low _____ steels are the ferrous materials that are
    gas welded most frequently.

18. As in aluminum welding, _____ is needed to break down surface oxides and ensure a sound weld.

19. The principle use of _____ solder in aircraft work is in the fabrication process of high

    pressure _____ lines.

20. The heat control of a TIG welder may be preset by a machine setting or variable by use of a _____

    _____ or a _____ control.

21. The grinding of a Tungsten electrode used in TIG welding should be done _____,

    not _____.

22. When welding aluminum the welding machine is set to an _____ output waveform because it

    causes a _____ that breaks up _____.

23. A good indication and measure of weld quality for titanium is the weld _____. A bright

    _____ weld indicates that the shielding is satisfactory.

24. What four types of welds commonly used in flat position welding:

    _____   _____

    _____   _____

25. Stresses developed by heating and cooling during welding need to be relieved or _____

    and _____ of the sheets will occur.

26. If a partial replacement of a tube is necessary, make an _____ sleeve splice, especially
    where you want a smooth tube surface.

27. Dents at a cluster weld can be repaired by welding a _____
    over the dented area.

28. A damaged tubular section can be repaired using welded _____ reinforcements.

29. The spring-steel part of a spring-steel leave is _____ and should not

    be _____ on.

30. The preferred method to repair an engine mount member is by using a _____
    replacement tube.

TRUE of FALSE

_____ 1. Friction stir welding is one of the most common welding techniques.

_____ 2. Gas welding was the most common welding method for thick (over 3/16") till the 1950s.

_____ 3. The temperature generated by SMAW is hotter than gas welding.

_____ 4. GMAW (MIG) welding is an improvement over SMAW (stick) welding.

_____ 5. GTAW (TIG) uses a consumable rod and a filler.

_____ 6. Plasma cutting systems can cut aluminum and stainless steel.

_____ 7. The acetylene pressure gauge should never be set higher than 20 psi for welding or cutting.

_____ 8. The acetylene hose is red and has left hand threads.

_____ 9. The flash back arrestor prevents the reverse flow of gas.

_____ 10. A backfire is a momentary backward flow of the gases at the torch tip.

_____ 11. Welding eyewear used for gas welding can also be used for arc welding processes.

_____ 12. Welding tips have a number of holes and cutting tips have one hole.

_____ 13. Open the torch oxygen valve a quarter to a half turn when lightening the torch.

_____ 14. The neutral flame burns higher than the carburizing flame. True/false

_____ 15. When shutting down the welding equipment the oxygen valve is closed first.

_____ 16. For welding thick metals or heavy plate, a technique called backhand welding can be used.

_____ 17. Maintain a slight excess of acetylene for most steels, and a neutral flame for stainless

_____ 18. Gas welding of some aluminum alloys can be accomplished successfully.

_____ 19. Welding magnesium is done with a slightly carburizing flame.

_____ 20. Pure tungsten electrodes have better electron emission characteristics than Thoriated electrodes.

_____ 21. When TIG welding aluminum the welding equipment is switched to a AC output waveform.

_____ 22. Tig welding of titanium is performed using AC straight polarity.

_____ 23. Expansion and contraction caused by heat during the welding process have a tendency to buckle and warp thin sheet metal sheets.

_____ 24. Tack welding at intervals of the joint could control the expansion of the sheets that are welded.

_____ 25. A damaged tubular section can be repaired using a formed steel patch plate.

Chapter 5, Section A - Aircraft Welding

name: _____

1. What is the preferred method of welding magnesium?

2. What is a safety hazard associated with welding magnesium?

3. What must be done in the weld zone to successfully weld titanium?

4. Why is it necessary to use flux in all silver soldering?

5. What type of flame is used for silver soldering?

6. What type of repair could be made for a dented steel tube cluster joint?

7. What method can be used to insert a tight fitting inner sleeve into a tubular repair?

8. How is a soft flame obtained without reducing thermal output?

9. What is the most extensively used method of welding aluminum?

10. What valve should be turned off first when extinguishing a torch?

11. What procedure will control expansion when welding a joint?

12. What safety precaution should be taken when gas welding has been completed?

13. What must be done with heat-treated aluminum alloys after a welding repair has been made?

14. What is the result of insufficient penetration?

15. What type of welding causes less buckling and warping than gas welding?

16. What is gas shielded arc welding?

17. What are some advantages of gas shielded arc welding?

1. Edge notching is generally recommended in butt welding above a certain thickness of aluminum because it:
    a. helps hold the metal in alignment during welding
    b. aids in the removal or penetration of oxides on the metal surface
    c. aids in getting full penetration of the metal and prevents local distortion

2. Which statement concerning a welding process is true?
    a. The inert arc welding process uses an inert gas to protect the weld zone from the atmosphere.
    b. In the metallic arc welding process, filler material, if needed, is provided by a separate metal rod of the proper material held in the arc
    c. In the oxyacetylene welding process, the filler rod used for steel is covered with a thin coating of flux

3. Where should the flux be applied when oxyacetylene welding aluminum?
    a. Painted only on the surface to be welded
    b. Painted on the surface to be welded and applied to the welding rod
    c. Applied only to the welding rod

4. What purpose does flux serve in welding aluminum?
    a. Removes dirt, grease, and oil
    b. Minimizes or prevents oxidation
    c. Ensures proper distribution of the filler rod

5. Why are aluminum plates 1/4 inch or more thick usually preheated before welding?
    a. Reduces internal stresses and assures more complete penetration
    b. Reduces welding time
    c. Prevents corrosion and ensures proper distribution of flux

6. How should a welding torch flame be adjusted to weld stainless steel?
    a. Slightly carburizing
    b. Slightly oxidizing
    c. Neutral

7. Oxides form rapidly when alloys or metals are hot. So it is important when welding aluminum to use a:
    a. solvent
    b. filler
    c. flux

8. In gas welding, the amount of heat applied to the material being welded is controlled by the
    a. amount of gas pressure used
    b. size of the tip opening
    c. distance the tip is held from the work

9. The shielding gases generally used in the Gas Tungsten Arc (GTA) welding of aluminum consist of
    a. a mixture of nitrogen and carbon dioxide
    b. nitrogen or hydrogen, or a mixture of nitrogen and hydrogen
    c. helium or argon, or a mixture of helium and argon

10. Acetylene at a line pressure above 15 PSI is
    a. dangerously unstable.
    b. used when a reducing flame is necessary.
    c. usually necessary when welding metal over 3/8-inch thick.

11. If too much acetylene is used in the welding of stainless steel,
    a. a porous weld will result
    b. the metal will absorb carbon and lose its resistance to corrosion
    c. oxide will be formed on the base metal close to the weld

12. In Gas Tungsten Arc (GTA) welding, a stream of inert gas is used to:
    a. prevent the formation of oxides in the puddle
    b. concentrate the heat of the arc and prevent its dissipation
    c. lower the temperature required to properly fuse the metal

13. When a butt welded joint is visually inspected for penetration?
    a. the penetration should be 25 to 50 percent of the thickness of the base metal
    b. the penetration should be 100 percent of the thickness of the base metal
    c. look for evidence of excessive heat in the form of a very high bead

14. Why is it necessary to use flux in all silver soldering operations?
    a. To chemically clean the base metal of oxide film
    b. To prevent overheating of the base metal
    c. To increase heat conductivity

15. A welding torch backfire may be caused by:
    a. a loose tip
    b. using too much acetylene
    c. a tip temperature that is too cool

16. Which statement best describes magnesium welding?
    a. Magnesium can be welded to other metals
    b. Filler rod should be nickel steel
    c. Filler rod should be the same composition as base metal

17. Engine mount members should preferably be repaired by using a:
    a. larger diameter tube with fishmouth and no rosette welds
    b. larger diameter tube with fishmouth and rosette welds
    c. smaller diameter tube with fishmouth and rosette welds

18. What method of repair is recommended for a steel tube longeron dented at a cluster?
    a. Welded split sleeve
    b. Welded outer sleeve
    c. Welded patch plate

19. Welding over brazed or soldered joints is:
    a. not permitted.
    b. permissible for mild steel.
    c. permissible for most metals or alloys that are not heat treated.

20. A resurfaced soldering iron cannot be used effectively until after the working face has been:
    a. fluxed
    b. polished
    c. tinned

21. In selecting a torch tip size to use in welding, the size of the tip opening determines the:
    a. amount of heat applied to the work
    b. temperature of the flame
    c. melting point of the filler metal

22. Why should a carburizing flame be avoided when welding steel?
    a. It removes the carbon content
    b. It hardens the surface
    c. A cold weld will result

23. The most important consideration(s) when selecting welding rod is:
    a. current setting or flame temperature
    b. material compatibility
    c. ambient conditions

24. A very thin and pointed tip on a soldering copper is undesirable because it will:
    a. transfer too much heat to the work
    b. have a tendency to overheat and become brittle
    c. cool too rapidly

25. Which statement is true in regard to welding heat-treated magnesium?
    a. The welded section does not have the strength of the original metal
    b. Flux should not be used because it is very difficult to remove and is likely to cause corrosion
    c. Magnesium cannot be repaired by fusion welding because of the high probability of igniting the metal

Chapter 6 - Aircraft Wood

Chapter 6 - Section A
Study Aid Questions

Fill in the Blanks

1. The ideal range of moisture content in a wood aircraft structure is _____ percent, with any readings

   over _____ percent providing an environment for the growth of fungus in the wood.

2. A good indication of moisture, fungal growth, and possible _____ is a _____

   or _____ odor.

3. Aircraft that are exposed to large cyclic changes of _____ and _____

   are especially prone to wood shrinkage that may lead to glue joint _____.

4. Glued joints are generally designed to take _____ loads.

5. Wood _____ and dry _____ are usually easy to detect.

   _____ may be evident as either a discoloration or a softening of the wood.

6. Dark discoloration or gray stains running along the grain are indicative of _____.

7. Inspect structural members for _____ failures, which is indicated by rupture across
   the wood fibers.

8. Tapping a wood structure with a light plastic hammer should produce a _____
   sound.

9. _____ is the preferred choice of wood and the standard by which the other wood
   types are measured.

10. All solid wood and _____ should be of the highest quality and grade.

11. All woods used for structural repair of aircraft are classified as _____.

12. Pin knot clusters are acceptable if they produce only a small effect on _____.

13. _____ are acceptable if careful inspection fails to reveal any decay.

14. Checks are longitudinal _____ extending, in general across the annual rings.

15. _____ wood is characterized by high specific gravity.

16. Some of the more common adhesives that have been used in aircraft construction and repair include

_____, _____

_____ and, _____ adhesives.

17. _____ are a useful means of detecting the presence of wax on a wood surface or joint.

18. Satisfactory glue joints in aircraft should develop the _____ of the wood under

all conditions of _____.

19. _____ are the most satisfactory method of fabricating an end joint between two solid members.

20. A damaged spar may be spliced at almost any point except at _____,

_____,

_____, or lift and interplane strut fittings.

TRUE or FALSE

_____ 1. A certificated mechanic who has not performed repairs to wooden aircraft before is not allowed to perform repairs to a wood aircraft structure.

_____ 2. When inspecting an aircraft constructed or comprised of wood components the moisture content must be above 20%.

_____ 3. Some slight sectional undulation or bulging between panels of aircraft using single plywood covering may be permissible if the wood and glue are sound.

_____ 4. Glued joints are generally designed to take bearing loads.

_____ 5. Dark discoloration of wood or gray stains running along the grain are indicative of water penetration.

_____ 6. The condition of the fabric covering on plywood surfaces does not provide an useful indication of the condition of the wood underneath.

_____ 7. Compression failures are indicated by rupture across the wood fibers.

_____ 8. When during an inspection of a wood structure a soft and mushy area is found, the mechanic should disassemble and repair that structure.

_____ 9. Douglas fir is the preferred choice of wood and the standard by which other woods are measured.

_____ 10. All woods used for structural repair of aircraft are classifies as hardwoods.

_____ 11. Wavy, curly, interlocked grain are acceptable, if local irregularities do not exceed limitations specified for spiral and diagonal grain.

_____ 12. Hard knots are not acceptable in wood species used for aircraft repair.

_____ 13. Checks, shakes, and splits are acceptable under certain conditions in wood repair.

_____ 14. Decay on aircraft wooden parts for repair are never acceptable.

_____ 15. Smooth even surfaces produced on planers and joiners with sharp knives and correct feed adjustments are the best surfaces for gluing solid wood.

_____ 16. The proper way to prepare wood surfaces is to sand the surface with a 180 grit sandpaper.

_____ 17. All gluing operations should be performed above 70 °F for proper performance of the adhesive.

_____ 18. The repairs to solid or laminated spars are never permitted and the spar should be replaced with a new spar from the manufacturer or the holder of a PMA for that part.

_____ 19. A fabric patch could be used to repair holes not exceeding 1 inch in diameter.

_____ 20. A properly prepared and installed scarf patch is the bests repair for damaged plywood and is preferred for most skin repairs.

name: _____

Knowledge Application Questions

1. Describe what a laminated wood assembly consists of?

2. How is aircraft plywood different from laminated wood?

3. What species of wood is used as a standard for strength properties?

4. How can rot be revealed during an inspection of a wood structure?

5. What types of glues are used in aircraft wood structure repair?

6. What effects do room temperature have on gluing wood structures using resin glue or epoxy adhesives?

7. Under what condition are mineral streaks acceptable?

8. Are hard knots acceptable in aircraft quality wood?

9. Explain why compressed wood is not acceptable for aircraft wood structures?

10. Why is it necessary to examine all stains and discoloration carefully?

11. Why are light steel bushings sometimes used in wooden structures?

12. What are the results of non-uniform gluing pressure?

13. Name three methods that are used to apply pressure to wood glue joints?

14. What is the most effective type of joint used in splicing structural members?

15. Why does the strength of a beveled scarf joint depend on the accuracy of the beveled cut?

16. Always splice and reinforce plywood webs with what type of wood?

17. What method will prevent a patch and a plywood pressure plate from adhering together due to extruding glue from the patch?

18. What areas of a wood spar may not be spliced?

19. Why are bushings made of plastic or light metal used on wooden structures?

20. What is the minimum temperature for curing wood joints with resin glue or epoxy adhesives?

1. Which statement about wood decay is correct?
    a. Decay that occurs before the wood is seasoned does not affect the strength of the finished piece.
    b. A limited amount of certain kinds of decay is acceptable in aircraft woods since decay affects the binding between the fibers and not the fibers themselves.
    c. Decay is not acceptable in any form or amount.

2. Compression failures in wood aircraft structures are characterized by buckling of the fibers that appear as streaks on the surface
    a. at right angles to the growth rings.
    b. parallel to the grain.
    c. at right angles to the grain.

3. Glue deterioration in wood aircraft structure is indicated
    a. when a joint has separated and the glue surface shows only the imprint of the wood with no wood fibers clinging to the glue.
    b. when a joint has separated and the glue surface shows pieces of wood or wood fibers clinging to the glue.
    c. by any joint separation.

4. When patching a plywood skin, abrupt changes in cross sectional areas which will develop dangerous stress concentration should be avoided by using
    a. circular or elliptical patches.
    b. square patches.
    c. doublers with any desired shaped patches.

5. Laminated wood is sometimes used in the construction of highly stressed aircraft components. This wood can be identified by its
    a. parallel grain construction.
    b. similarity to standard plywood construction.
    c. perpendicular grain construction.

6. Pin knot clusters are permitted in wood aircraft structure provided
    a. they produce a small effect on grain direction.
    b. they have no mineral streaks.
    c. no pitch pockets are within 12".

7. Which of the following conditions will determine acceptance of wood with mineral streaks?
    a. Careful inspection fails to reveal any decay.
    b. They produce only a small effect on grain direction.
    c. Local irregularities do not exceed limitations specified for spiral and diagonal grain.

8. A faint line running across the grain of a wood spar generally indicates
    a. compression failure.
    b. shear failure.
    c. decay.

9. In cases of elongated bolt holes in a wood spar or cracks in the vicinity of bolt holes,
    a. it is permissible to ream the hole, plug with hardwood, and redrill.
    b. the spar may be reinforced by using hardwood reinforcing plates.
    c. a new section of spar should be spliced in or the spar replaced entirely.

10. Where is information found concerning acceptable species substitutions for wood materials used in aircraft repair?
    a. Aircraft Specifications or Type Certificate Data Sheets.
    b. Technical Standard Orders.
    c. AC 43.13-1B.

11. The strength of a well designed and properly prepared wood splice joint is provided by the:
    a. bearing surface of the wood fibers.
    b. glue.
    c. reinforcement plates.

12. The I beam wooden spar is routed to:
    a. increase strength.
    b. obtain uniform strength.
    c. reduce weight.

name: _____

Chapter 7 - Composites

Chapter 7 - Section A
Study Aid Questions

Fill in the Blanks

1. What are the three primary advantages of composite materials?

2. Name five applications of composites on aircraft.

   _

3. List the two major components of a laminate.

4. List four examples of honey comb structures on aircraft.

5. List four advantages of Thermoplastic honeycomb material.

6. What are two advantages to using Polystyrene in sandwich structures?

7. List four composite manufacturing defects.

8. List four sources of composite manufacturing defects.

9. Matrix cracks, or micro cracks, can significantly reduce properties dependant on the resin or the fiber/resin

   interface, such as   and

10. List three types of damage to the composite surface that is detectable via a visual inspection.

11. List four types of discrepancies that can be detected with a visual inspection.

12. The signal from an unflawed region is used for   and any

   deviation from this unflawed signal (period) indicates the existence of

13. List four contaminants that prepreg materials must be protected from.

14. _____ utilizes precured composite detail parts, and uses a layer of adhesive to bond two procured composite parts.

15. Precured laminates undergoing secondary bonding usually have a thin _____ or

    _____ peel ply cured onto the bonding surface.

16. List 3 advantages of using composite doublers to repair metal skin components.

17. List the four types of bleed out techniques.

18. A temporary repair must meet the _____ but is limited by time or flight cycles.

19. A _____ repair can be used to repair damage to a sandwich honeycomb structure.

20. Water in the honeycomb core could _____ at high altitudes.

21. Sold laminate structures have _____ plies than the face sheets of honeycomb structures.

22. Resin injection repairs are used on _____ structures for _____ damages to a solid laminate.

23. Aircraft radomes are made of _____ material.

24. The properties of a _____ repair are not as good as a repair with

    _____ material, but by using a _____ method

    the properties of a _____ can be improved.

25. The disadvantage of bonded repairs is that most repair materials require _____

_____, and _____ procedures.

26. Bolted repairs are not desirable for _____ structure due to the thin

face sheets that have limited _____ strength.

27. Most composite primary structures for the aircraft industry are fastened with _____ or

_____ fasteners

28. Drill bits used for carbon fiber and fiber glass are made from _____ material or

_____ because the fibers are so hard that _____
drill bits will not last very long.

29. Countersinking a composite structure is required when _____ fasteners are used.

30. Drilling in composite material require _____speeds and _____
feeds than drilling in metallic structures.

TRUE or FALSE

_____ 1. Composite materials consist of a combination of materials that are mixed together to achieve specific
structural properties.

_____ 2. The Fibers in a composite are the primary load carrying element of the composite material.

_____ 3. Kevlar yarns are twisted, while Fiberglass yarns are not.

_____ 4. Unidirectional Tape Fibers are held in place by stitching with fine yards or threads and have a higher
strength than woven fabrics.

_____ 5. Satin Weaves have less crimp and are easier to distort than a plain weave

_____ 6. Special scissors are needed to cut Aramid Fibers

_____ 7. If the graphene layers or planes stack with 3 dimensional order, the material is defined as graphite.

_____ 8. Carbon Fibers have a low potential for causing galvanic corrosion when used with metallic fasteners
and structures.

_____ 9. Thermoplastic materials can repeatedly be softened by an increase of temperature and hardened by a
decrease in temperature.

_____ 10. Sandwich construction has high bending stiffness at minimal weight in comparison to aluminum and composite laminate construction.

_____ 11. Aluminum has the best strength-to-weight ration and energy absorption of all the materials used for honeycomb.

_____ 12. Bisected hexagonal honeycomb is stiffer and stronger than hexagonal core.

_____ 13. Aircraft grade Polystyrene has a tight closed cell structure with no voids between the cells.

_____ 14. Matrix imperfections may develop into delimitations, which are a more critical type of damage.

_____ 15. Visual inspections can not find internal flaws in the composite, such as delaminations, disbands, and matrix crazing.

_____ 16. When performing an Audible Sonic Test, the tapping rate needs to be slow enough to produce enough sound such that any difference in sound tone is discernable to the ear.

_____ 17. When using the Through Transmission Ultrasonic inspection method, areas without a signal loss compared to the reference standard indicate a defective area.

_____ 18. The mechanical life is shorter than the handling life.

_____ 19. Adhesive film is frequently placed into the interface between the stiffener and the skin to increase fatigue and peel resistance.

_____ 20. Composite Materials can be used to structurally repair, restore, or enhance aluminum, steel, and titanium components.

_____ 21. Too many bleeder plies can result in a resin rich repair.

_____ 22. Many high strength prepreg materials in use today are no-bleed systems.

_____ 23. Potted repairs do not restore the full strength of the part.

_____ 24. Water or moisture in honeycomb structures does not affect the structure during repair.

_____ 25. A scarf repair is more efficiently in load transfer than an external bonded patches.

_____ 26. Aircraft radomes are made of at least 10 plies of Kevlar.

_____ 27. The double Vacuum Debulk process will improve properties of a wet lay up repair.

_____ 28. Bonded repairs are quicker and easier to carry out than bolted repairs.

_____ 29. Titanium or stainless steel fasteners are used for bolted repairs of carbon fiber structure.

_____ 30. Sickle shaped Klenk drills are used to drill carbon fiber.

1. Describe the term *Homogeneous* as it applies to laminate structures.

2. Describe the term *Anisotropic* as it applies to laminate structures.

—

3. Describe the term *Quasi-isotropic* as it applies to laminate structures:

4. What benefit do most fabric constructions offer that straight unidirectional tapes do not?

5. What is a benefit of tightly woven fabrics on aerospace structures?

6. Name one type of conductive material used to protect composite components against lightening strikes?

7. Why are Phenolic resins used for interior components?

8. How many stages are there to curing resins and what are they?

9. Briefly explain why prepreg materials must be kept in a freezer at zero degrees Fahrenheit.

10. Bell shaped core cells, or flexicore, is used for what applications?

11. Explain what the benefits are for using honeycomb with a high density and small core cells.

12. Describe what it means for a part to be resin rich.

13. Describe what it means for a part to be resin starved.

14. Briefly explain the Audible Sonic Testing method.

15. Describe the sound indicative of a well-bonded solid structure when utilizing the Audible Sonic Testing method.

16. Describe the sound indicative of a discrepant area when utilizing the Audible Sonic Testing Method.

17. Describe what could produce a faulty result when utilizing the Audible sonic test.

18. Briefly describe how the Through Transmission Ultrasonic inspection method works.

19. If a clean room is not available for prepreg material lay-up, what techniques are used to prevent contamination?

20. What is co-curing and describe a typical co-cure application?

21. What is the difference between a permanent repair and an interim repair?

22. What is the restriction of potted repair related to flight controls?

23. Why does water/moisture needs to be removed before a repair to a honeycomb part is cured?

24. Explain the resin injection repair method

25. Describe why aircraft radomes need to be made of only 3 or 4 plies of fiberglass.

26. Describe in detail the Double Vacuum Debulk repair process.

1. What is the role of the Matrix component in the composite material?
   a. The Matrix is the primary load carrying element
   b. The Matrix supports the fibers and bonds them together
   c. The Matrix determines the direction that the composite material will be strongest
   d. The Matrix is the stacking sequence of the individual composite plies.

2. What do the structural properties such as stiffness, dimensional stability, and strength of a composite laminate depend on?
   a. The curing temperature
   b. The size of the fibers
   c. The stacking sequence of the plies
   d. The Matrix

3. In this ply orientation, the plies are stacked in a 0, -45, 45 and 90 degrees sequence or in a 0,-60 and +60 degree sequences. These types of ply orientation simulate the properties of an isotropic material.
   a. Bi-Directional
   b. Quasi-Isotropic
   c. Isotropic
   d. Unidirectional

4. What is an individual Fiber called?
   a. Splice
   b. Roving
   c. Filament
   d. Tape

5. What three terms are commonly used to describe a bundle of filaments?
   a. Strands, Tows, Rope
   b. Tows, Yarns, Roving
   c. Yarns, Strands, Tows
   d. Rope, Roving, Splice

6. Unidirectional tape products have which of the following physical properties?
   a. High shear strength perpendicular to the fiber direction
   b. High compressive strength across the fibers
   c. High tensile strength in the fiber direction
   d. High shear and compressive strength in the fiber direction

7. Kevlar is DuPont's trademark name for what type of fibers?
   a. Thermoplastics
   b. Polyester
   c. Carbon
   d. Aramid

8. What is the primary disadvantage of Aramid Fibers?
   a. Highly susceptible to impact damage
   b. Weak in compression
   c. Hygroscopic
   d. Both b and c

9. If the graphene layers or planes stack with a two dimensional order, the material is defined as:
   a. Carbon
   b. Graphite
   c. Aramid
   d. Fiberglass

10. What is required for aircraft carbon fiber parts that are prone to lightening strike?
    a. Lightening Rods
    b. Strapping to non-conductive aircraft parts
    c. Alternating aluminum plies
    d. Lightening protection mesh or coating

11. What are Ceramic fibers used for on aircraft?
    a. Propellers
    b. Turbine blades
    c. Compressor Blades
    d. Exhaust Nozzles

12. What cure temperature do Polyamides require?
    a. High cure temperatures in excess of 350 Degrees Fahrenheit
    b. High cure temperatures in excess of 450 Degrees Fahrenheit
    c. High cure temperatures in excess of 550 Degrees Fahrenheit
    d. High cure temperatures in excess of 650 Degrees Fahrenheit

13. Where are Bismaleimide (BMI) resins used?
    a. Aero engines
    b. High temperature components
    c. Control surfaces
    d. Both a and b

14. Most honeycomb materials are _____; that is, properties are directional.
    a. Anisotropic
    b. Isotropic
    c. Quasi-isotropic
    d. Heterogeneous

15. Honeycomb core cells for aerospace applications are typically what shape?
    a. Pentagons
    b. Diamonds
    c. Octagons
    d. Hexagons

16. What shape are honeycomb over-expanded core cells?
    a. Pentagons
    b. Hexagons
    c. Rectangles
    d. Octagons

17. What is considered to be the optimal fiber to resin ratio?
    a. 40:60
    b. 60:40
    c. 70:30
    d. 30:70

18. What causes delaminations to form?
    a. Matrix cracks that grow into the interlaminar layer
    b. Low energy impact
    c. Production non-adhesion along the bond line
    d. All of the Above

19. What type of inspection is the primary method for in-service inspections of composite materials?
    a. Audible Sonic Testing
    b. Visual
    c. Automated Tap Testing
    d. Ultrasonic

20. On what type of composite structure is tap testing most effective?
    a. Thin skin to stiffer bond lines
    b. Honeycomb sandwich with thin face sheets
    c. Near the surface of thick laminates
    d. All of the above

21. What Ultrasonic Inspection method uses two transducers, one on each side of the area to be inspected?
    a. Through Transmission
    b. Pulse Echo
    c. Ultrasonic Bond tester
    d. Phased Array

22. What Ultrasonic Inspection method uses a single search unit as a transmitting and receiving transducer that is excited by high voltage pulses?
    a. Through Transmission
    b. Pulse Echo
    c. Ultrasonic Bond tester
    d. Phased Array

23. What type of inspection is the primary method for in-service inspections of composite materials?
    a. Audible Sonic Testing
    b. Visual
    c. Automated Tap Testing
    d. Ultrasonic

24. What is the typical storage life for prepreg material?
    a. 2 to 8 months
    b. 4 to 10 months
    c. 6 to 12 months
    d. 8 to 14 months

25. What is used to improve the peel strength of Co-bonded assemblies?
    a. Boron Prepreg tape
    b. Film Adhesive
    c. Silicon Adhesive
    d. Enhanced Epoxy resin

26. What is considered to be a permanent repair?
    a. Meet the strength requirements but is limited by time of flight cycles
    b. Meet the strength requirements but has a different inspection schedule
    c. Meet the strength requirements and the durability requirements
    d. b and c are correct

27. A potted repair should not be used for _____?
    a. Small repairs to honey comb structure
    b. Small repairs to honey comb engine cowlings
    c. Small repairs to honey comb flight controls
    d. Small repairs to honey comb spoilers

28. Scarf type repairs use _____ scarf angles to ease the load into the repair.
    a. large
    b. small
    c. scarf angle does not affect the load
    d. depends on the repair material

29. What condition could affect the signal of the aircraft radar?
    a. Trapped water in the aircraft radome
    b. Large potted repairs of the aircraft radome
    c. a and b are both correct
    d. a and b are both wrong

30. Honeycomb sandwich structures are often repaired with
    a. Scarf type bonded repair
    b. Scarf type bolted repair
    c. An external bolted repair
    d. An internal bonded repair

Chapter 8 - Aircraft Painting

Chapter 8 - Section A
Study Aid Questions

Fill in the Blanks

1 Paint is more than aesthetics, it affects the _____ of the aircraft and protects

   the _____ of the airframe.

2. _____ is at the top of the list when compared to other coatings for
   abrasion, stain, and chemical resistant properties.

3. There are several methods of applying aircraft finish. Among the most common are: _____

   _____, and _____.

4. There are two main types of spray equipment: _____

   and _____.

5. The three most common types of spray guns used are: _____

   _____, and _____.

6. The HVLP production spray gun is an _____ mix gun. The _____

   and _____ is mixed inside the air cap.

7. The most important part of any painting project is the _____.

8. The _____ control knob of a spray gun controls the airflow (pattern shape)

9. Primer is typically applied using a _____ spray pattern.

10. While painting the second pass will overlap the first pass by _____ percent.

11. A quick check of the spray pattern can be verified by spraying some _____ or

_____ through the gun.

12. A pulsating, or spitting fan pattern may be caused by a _____, _____

vent hole on the supply cup, or the _____may be leaking around the needle.

13. Blushing is the dull _____ that appears in a paint finish.

14. Pin holes are the result of _____, _____

or _____.

15. Sags and runs are caused by applying _____ paint to an area, by holding the spray

gun _____ to the surface, or moving the gun _____
across the surface.

16. Orange peel refers to the appearance of a _____ surface.

17. Fisheyes appear as _____ in the coating as it is being applied.

18. Wrinkling is usually caused by _____ and _____
of the paint finish due to excessively thick or solvent heavy paint coats

19. Spray dust could be caused by spray gun held _____ from the surface, or

incorrect spray gun _____.

20. For a spot repair that requires blending of the coating, an area about _____ times
the area of the actual repair must be prepared.

TRUE or FALSE

_____ 1. The top coat applied to external parts of the aircraft protect against corrosion and deterioration.

_____ 2. Epoxy primer is recommended for steel tube frame aircraft prior to installing fabric covering.

_____ 3. Older type zinc chromate primers are distinguishable by its flat green color.

_____ 4. If the paint materials are too thick, they are likely to run or not cover the surface adequately.

_____ 5. A HVLP spray gun transfers more paint to the surface of the painted surface.

_____ 6. The HVLP spray gun is an external mix gun.

_____ 7. Fresh air breathing systems should be used when spraying polyurethane paint because it contains isocyanides

_____ 8. The Zahn cup is used to measure the viscosity of the primer or paint system.

_____ 9. Alodine is not used with aluminum aircraft, it is mostly used with composite aircraft structures.

_____ 10. The upper control knob of the paint gun controls the airflow and the bottom control knob controls the fluid flow.

_____ 11. If the spray pattern is offset to one side or the other, the fluid valve may be plugged.

_____ 12. A spitting fan pattern may be caused by a loose nozzle, clogged vent hole or a leaking packing.

_____ 13. When painting an aircraft, start painting the large surfaces first and than fill in the corners and gaps.

_____ 14. Blushing is the dull milky haze that appears in a paint finish.

_____ 15. Orange peel could be caused by not enough reducer or too little flash time between coats.

_____ 16. The most effective way to eliminate fisheyes is to ensure that the temperature is above 70 °F.

_____ 17. Each operator of an aircraft shall display on the aircraft, marks consisting of the Roman capital letter "U" (denoting United States registration).

_____ 18. The registration marks must be at least 10 inches high. A glider may display marks at least 3 inches.

_____ 19. One way to test if the old paint is to apply turbine oil to a small area. If the paint softens within a few minutes the paint system is an acrylic or epoxy paint finish.

_____ 20. Plastic Media Blasting (PMB) is an effective way of stripping paint of composite structures which causes less damage than sanding.

1. What are the common types of paint used on aircraft?

2. Why are old zinc type primers (bright yellow color) not used anymore for modern aircraft.

3. What will happen if the ports in the horn of the spray gun aircap are becoming plugged?

4. What is the purpose of primers?

    .

5. Many of the solvents and thinners used in modern finishing systems are toxic; what health safety precaution should the mechanic observe?

6. What are three methods of applying paint?

7. What is the cause for spray dust?

8. What may cause spray paint sags and runs?

9. What causes orange peel spray mottle?

10. What is a blushing paint finish?

11. What will cause a blushing paint finish?

12. What could be the result of applying a coat of paint when the temperature of the dope room is too high?

13. What areas must be protected from damage when using paint remover/stripper?

14. What is the reason for paint touchup other than appearance?

15. What is the most common finish system for modern transport category aircraft?

16. Name three ways to strip paint from an aircraft

17. Describe how to adjust a spray gun for painting large surfaces.

18. What could cause a pulsating or spitting fan pattern?

19. What is the most effective way to eliminate fisheyes?

20. What is the location of the registration mark on fixed wing aircraft?

1. Which of the following is a hazard associated with sanding on fabric surfaces during the finishing process?
   a. Overheating of the fabric/finish, especially with the use of power tools.
   b. Static electricity buildup.
   c. Embedding of particles in the finish.

2. What is likely to occur if unhydrated wash primer is applied to unpainted aluminum and then about 30 to 40 minutes later a finish topcoat, when the humidity is low?
   a. Corrosion.
   b. A glossy, blush-free finish.
   c. A dull finish due to the topcoat 'sinking in' to primer that is still too soft.

3. Before applying a protective coating to any unpainted clean aluminum, you should
   a. wipe the surface with avgas or kerosene.
   b. remove any conversion coating film.
   c. avoid touching the surface with bare hands.

4. What is the usual cause of runs and sags in aircraft finishes?
   a. Too much material applied in one coat.
   b. Material is being applied too fast.
   c. Low atmospheric humidity.

5. Which defect in aircraft finishes may be caused by adverse humidity, drafts, or sudden changes in temperature?
   a. Orange peel.
   b. Blushing.
   c. Pinholes.

6. If masking tape is left on for several days and/or exposed to heat, it is likely that the tape will
   a. not seal out the finishing material if the delay or heating occurs before spraying.
   b. be weakened in its ability to adhere to the surface.
   c. cure to the finish and be very difficult to remove.

7. What is used to slow the drying time of some finishes and to prevent blush?
   a. Reducer.
   b. Retarder.
   c. Rejuvenator.

8. Which type of coating typically includes phosphoric acid as one of its components at the time of application?
   a. Wash primer.
   b. Epoxy primer.
   c. Zinc chromate primer.

9. Which properly applied finish topcoat is the most durable and chemical resistant?
   a. Synthetic enamel.
   b. Acrylic lacquer.
   c. Polyurethane.

10. Aluminum-pigment in dope is used primarily to
    a. provide a silver color
    b. aid in sealing out moisture from the fabric
    c. exclude sunlight from the fabric

11. What could happen if the to be painted surface is not clean and free of any type of contaminants?
    a. The surface has the appearance of orange peel
    b. The surface feels rough
    c. Fisheyes could appear on the surface

12. A rough surface that feels like sandpaper is an indication of?
    a. spray dust
    b. orange peel
    c. fisheyes

13. What could happen if the paint material is not properly mixed?
    a. fisheyes
    b. orange peel
    c. wrinkles

14. The registration marks must be at least _____ inches high. A glider may display marks at least _____ inches.
    a. 8 inches, 4 inches
    b. 10 inches, 6 inches
    c. 12 inches, 3 inches

15. The pressure used for a HVLP spray gun is _____ the pressure used for a traditional spray gun.
    a. lower than
    b. higher than
    c. equal to

16. A spray gun that uses lower pressure and higher volumes of air is called a:
    a. HVLP spray gun
    b. Siphon feed gun
    c. Gravity feed gun

17. With 12" high registration marks, what is the minimum space required for the registration mark N1683C?

    Notes: 2/3 x height = character width   1/6 x height = width for 1
             1/4 x 2/3 height = spacing   1/6 x height = stroke or line width
    a. 52 inches
    b. 48 inches
    c. 57 inches

Chapter 9 - Electrical

Chapter 9 - Section A
Study Aid Questions

Fill in the Blanks

1. Ohm's Law describes the basic _____ relationships of _____.

2. Materials with a resistance to current flow halfway between the best conductor and the best insulators are

   called _____. Their application is in the field of _____.

3. Almost all mechanical devices, such as _____ and _____,
   use electromagnetic induction to produce electrical power.

4. According to Fleming's left hand rule the thumb represents _____, the index

   finger represents _____, and the middle finger denotes _____.

5. DC systems that require AC current use a(n) _____ to make the switch from 24-volt DC

   to 400 _____ current in order to operate specialty equipment.

6. _____ reactance and _____ reactance oppose

   current flow in AC circuits. They may also create a _____ shift between voltage and current.

7. Capacitance of parallel plates is _____ proportional to the distance between the plates.

   Therefore, if the distance doubles the capacitance is _____ by _____.

8. In an AC circuit where there is no inductance or capacitance, _____ is equal to the

   _____ of the circuit.

9. Two main types of batteries include _____ and _____. They are

   identified by the material used for the _____.

10. The emergency rate is the total _____ load required to support the essential bus for

    _____ minutes.

11. Unlike lead-acid batteries, the state of charge of a Ni-Cad battery cannot be determined by measuring the

    specific gravity of the _____ electrolyte. State of charge is found by

    measuring the _____ with a Ni-Cad battery charger and following the

    _____.

12. In a series wound DC generator, when load increases, the voltage _____. This is

    because the greater the current through the field coils to the external circuit, the _____

    the induced EMF and the _____ the output voltage.

13. DC generator control systems are often referred to as voltage regulators or _____.

    They are designed to keep the generator _____ within limits for all flight condition.

14. DC alternators contain two major components including the _____ winding and

    the _____ winding. Using the process of _____ induction,

    voltage is produced and fed to the aircraft electrical _____ and current is

    produced to power any electrical _____.

15. A solid state regulator monitors DC alternator output _____ and controls alternator

    _____ current.

16. Inverters are _____ devices that convert DC power to _____.

    DC power feeds power to an AC distribution _____ that can be either 26 or 115 volts.

17. Constant speed drives can either be an independent unit or mounted within the _____.

    A dual CSD and alternator is known as a(n) _____.

18. AC alternator controls that measure the integrity of the electrical system include the _____

    (BPCU) and the _____ (GCU).

19. A warning horn, with the gear switch in the up position, sounds when the _____

    is reduced past a certain threshold and when the gear squat switch is _____.

20. Due to inflight vibration and _____, conductor wire should be _____
    to minimize fatigue breakage.

21. Insulation resistance can be measured with a _____ or insulation tester, although

    it may not give a true picture of the _____ of the insulation.

22. The amount of current _____ is a function of the number of wires in the bundle and

    the _____ of the total wire bundle capacity that is being used.

23. Circuit resistance can be determined by checking the _____ across the circuit. As

    long as this value does not exceed the limit set down by the manufacturer, the resistance value for the circuit

    is considered _____.

24. There should be no more than _____ splice(s) in any one wire segment between two connectors.

    Splices in bundles must be _____ as to minimize any increase in bundle size.

25. _____ are devices that open and close circuits and they consist of one or more

    pair of contacts. Current is permitted to flow when these contacts _____ .

1. Match these diagram types with their descriptions below

      a. wiring diagrams   *b. block diagrams*   *c. pictorial diagrams*   *d. schematic diagrams*

_____ 1. Picture of the components used instead of conventional electrical symbols

_____ 2. Indicates the location of components with respect to each other

_____ 3. Consists of blocks that represent several components

_____ 4. Illustrates principle of operation

_____ 5. Identifies each component within a system by its part and serial number

_____ 6. Aid in troubleshooting complex electrical systems

2.   Match these switch types with their descriptions below.

          a. switches   *b. electromagnetic switches*   *c. current limiters*

_____ 1. Double-pole single-throw   _____ 2. Relay

_____ 3. Solenoid   _____ 4. Fuse

_____ 5. Toggle and rocker   _____ 6. Circuit breaker

3. Match these switch types with the description or diagram below.

        a. SPST   *b. DPST*   *c. SPDT*   *d. DPDT*

_____ 1. Switch is on in both positions

_____ 2. Activates two separate circuits at the same time

_____ 3. Switch routes current through either of the two paths

_____ 4. Turns two circuits ON & OFF with one lever

_____ 5. Open and closes a single circuit

_____ 6. May have a center "OFF" position

_____ 7.   _____ 8.

_____ 9.   _____ 10.

4. Match these aircraft lighting types with the descriptions below.

        a. anti-collision lights   *b. position lights*   *c. landing and taxi lights*

        d. wing   *e. inspection lights*

_____ 1. Lights positioned in recessed areas of the wing designed to illuminate the ground

_____ 2. Rotating beam lights installed on the top of the fuselage or tail

_____ 3. Consists of one red, one green, and one white light

_____ 4. Lights that illuminate the leading edge of the wings

_____ 5. Has a white light located on the vertical stabilizer

_____ 6. Considered a safety light

_____ 7. Very powerful light directed by a parabolic reflector

5. Match these functions with their descriptions below.

        a. Voltage Regulation   *b. Overvoltage Protection*   *c. Parallel Gen. Operations*

        d. Over-excitation Protection   *e. Differential Voltage*   *f. Reverse Current Sensing*

_____ 1. Ensures all generator voltage values are w/in a close tolerance before load is brought online

_____ 2. Adjusts the voltage regulation circuit to ensure all generators operate w/in limits

_____ 3. Adjusts field current to control generator output

_____ 4. Disconnects a generator from a bus in the event it becomes inoperative

_____ 5. Controls a generator that is out of limits due to a paralleled system failure

_____ 6. Opens the relay that controls the field excitation current

6. Place the order of sequence of these events from start to finish. (from a – f)

_____ 1. pilot exciter field creates a magnetic field and induces power in the pilot exciter field

_____ 2. via EMF, main alternator field generates power in the main armature

_____ 3. output of exciter armature is rectified

_____ 4. ACU receives power output from 1 of the armatures and sends it to the exciter field

_____ 5. output of main AC armature is 3 phase AC

_____ 6. exciter permanent magnet and armature start process

----

1. A circuit with a 10Ω lamp and a 24 V DC battery has a current of how many amps?

2. What is the resistance of a lamp in a circuit with a 12 V DC battery and a current value of 3 amps?

3. What is the system voltage of a circuit with a resistance of 3.5Ω and a total current of 6.85A?

4. What is the effective value of the voltage if the peak value is 24V?

5. What is the peak value of the voltage if the effective voltage is 112V?

—

6. Referring to the diagram below; in an AC circuit with an inductance value of .175 Henrys and voltage of 110V at 60 cycles per second, what is the inductive reactance?

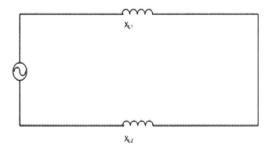

7. Referring to the diagram below, what is the impedance of the following circuit?

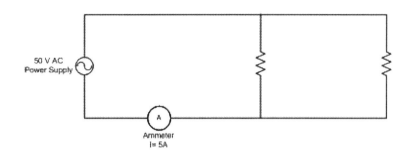

8. Referring to the diagram below and the relationship between impedance, resistance, and reactance, find the total impedance of the following circuit.

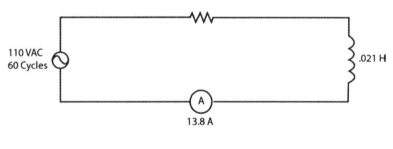

9. Referring to the diagram below; find the total impedance of the following circuit.

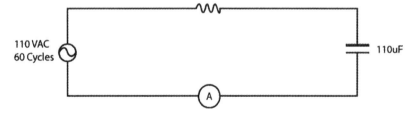

10. What is the equation for true power? _____

11. What is the unit for T.P.? _____

12. Referring to the diagram below, what is the total impedance of the following parallel AC circuit?

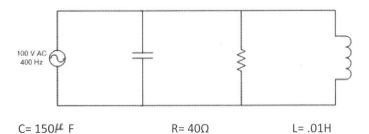

C= 150µ F   R= 40Ω   L= .01H

_____

13. What is the equation for apparent power? _____

14. What is the unit for A.P.? _____

15. Referring to the circuit diagram below, find TP, AP, and PF.   (R$_T$=5.6Ω)

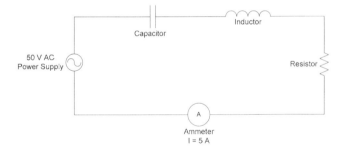

_____

16. Using below chart - fig. 11-2; determine the wire size for the following conditions:
    -voltage source 115 volt, continuous operation
    -conduit
    -wire run of 160ft
    -10A load capacity

    _____

17. Using below chart - fig. 11-2; determine the wire size considering the following:
    -voltage source 14V, continuous operation
    -conduit
    -wire run length of 7ft
    -7A load capacity

    _____

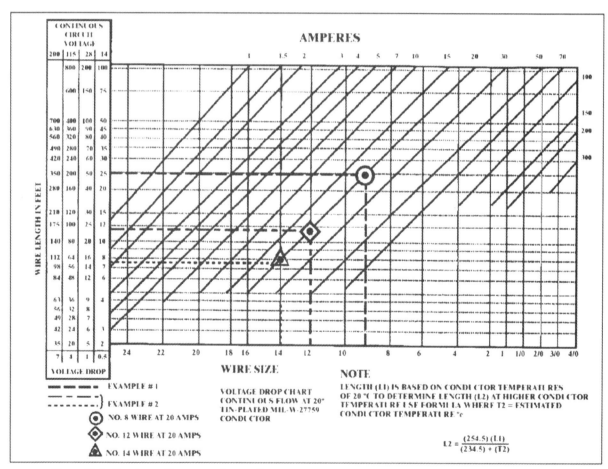

Figure 11-2   Conductor Chart – continuous flow

18. Using the below chart – fig. 11-3; determine the wire size considering the following:
    -Voltage 28V, intermittent flow   -conduit
    -wire run of 24'   -10A load

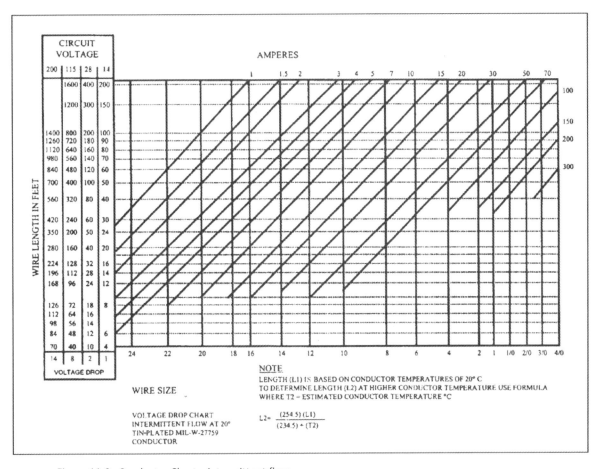

Figure 11-2   Conductor Chart – intermittent flow

19. Using below chart - fig. 11-4; What is the free air rating of a size 18 wire at an ambient temperature of 70°C and rated at 195°C?
   195-70=125, wire size 18

20. Using below chart - fig. 11-4; What is the free air rating of a #22 wire at an ambient temperature of 40°C and rated at 200°C?
   200-40=160, wire size 22

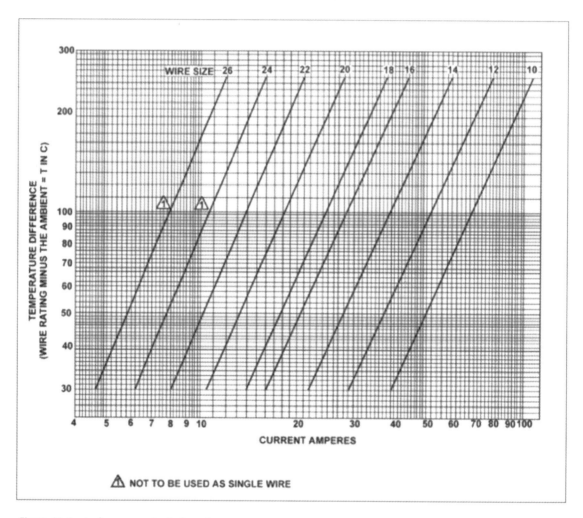

Figure 11-4   single copper wire in free air

1. What does Ohm's law state?
    a. the <u>current</u> through a conductor is directly <u>proportional</u> to the voltage applied to that conductor, and inversely proportional to the <u>resistance</u> of the conductor.
    b. the <u>current</u> through a conductor is inversely <u>proportional</u> to the voltage applied to that conductor, and directly proportional to the <u>resistance</u> of the conductor.
    c. the <u>current</u> through a conductor is directly <u>proportional</u> to the voltage applied to that conductor and proportional to the <u>resistance</u> of the conductor.
    d. the <u>current</u> through a conductor is inversely <u>proportional</u> to the voltage applied to that conductor and proportional to the <u>resistance</u> of the conductor.

2. What is voltage?
    a. electrical pressure
    b. force
    c. both A &B
    d. none of the above

3. Which of the following is a general rule regarding resistance in a circuit.
    a. The lesser the resistance, the lesser the current flow.
    b. The greater the resistance, the lesser the current flow.
    c. The greater the resistance, the greater the current flow.
    d. The resistance does not affect the current flow only voltage does.

4. What is the relationship between resistance and the length of a metallic conductor ?
    a. directly proportional
    b. indirectly proportional
    c. no relationship

5. What determines the polarity within the conductor?
                    I. direction in which the wire is moved
                II. position of the north and south poles of the field
            III. the speed in which the conductor is moved through the magnets
    a. only I
    b. only II
    c. both I & II
    d. both II & III

6. The effective value in an AC system has the same value as which of the following.
    a. DC voltage of the same value
    b. peak values of the sine wave
    c. the root mean square of the instantaneous voltage
    d. 1.41 x peak voltage

7. What is the relationship between period and frequency?
    a. P is inversely proportional to f
    b. f is inversely proportional to P
    c. P is equal to f^2
    d. f is equal to P^2

8. What are the terms used to describe wave lengths that are out of phase with one another?
   a. lead and lag
   b. forward and aft
   c. positive and negative
   d. no terms, just denoted in degrees out of phase

9. What is resistance's relationship to current and voltage, respectively?
   a. inversely to current and inversely to voltage
   b. inversely to current and directly to voltage
   c. directly to current and inversely to voltage
   d. directly to current and directly to voltage

10. What is inductance?
    a. a coils ability to resist any change in current through it
    b. a coils ability to hold an electric charge
    c. the total opposition to current flow

11. What is the relationship of inductive reactance to inductance and frequency, respectively?
    a. indirectly proportional, indirectly proportional
    b. indirectly proportional, directly proportional
    c. directly proportional, directly proportional
    d. directly proportional, indirectly proportional

12. What is the purpose of a capacitor in an electric circuit?
    a. reduces the inductive reactance
    b. reservoir that stores electricity
    c. opposes the flow of current
    d. increases the voltage

13. What is capacitive reactance?
    a. the opposition to current flow due to the rate of charge of the circuit
    b. rate of charge of the circuit
    c. the phase shift caused by the charging of a capacitor

14. Which of the following is NOT a part of impedance?
    a. resistance
    b. current
    c. inductive reactance
    d. capacitive reactance

15. What is a dry charged cell battery?
    a. one that is known as flooded or wet
    b. one that has been discharged before it was recharged
    c. one that does not require an electrolyte
    d. one that has 6 cells for an open circuit voltage of 24V

16. How much voltage does each cell in a Ni-Cad battery deliver during discharge?
    a. 1.2V
    b. 1.4V
    c. 2.0V
    d. 2.4V

17. Ni-Cad batteries typically have a fault protection system that monitors the condition of the battery, what does it monitor?

    | I. overheat condition | II. low heat condition |
    | III. cell imbalance | IV. open and short circuit |

    a. I & II only
    b. I & III only
    c. III & IV only
    d. all of the above

18. How can the overall battery condition be checked?
    a. load check
    b. closed circuit voltage
    c. resistance check
    d. opens circuit current rating

19. What charging method is preferred for lead-acid batteries?
    a. constant current
    b. constant voltage
    c. varying current
    d. varying voltage

20. What is the benefit of the constant current charging method?
    a. prolongs the life of the battery
    b. there is no potential for the battery to overheat or gas excessively
    c. fastest charging method for aircraft batteries
    d. multiple batteries of varying voltages can be charged together

21. What charging method is preferred for Ni-Cad batteries?
    a. constant current
    b. constant voltage
    c. varying current
    d. varying voltage

22. Where is the voltage induced in a DC generator?
    a. armature
    b. slip rings
    c. stator
    d. brushes

23. Which of these is NOT a major part of a DC generator?
    a. field frame
    b. field winding
    c. rotating armature
    d. brush assembly

24. Why are the poles laminated?
    a. reduce eddy current loses
    b. reduces arching
    c. prolongs the life of poles

25. How is the compound DC generator connected?
    a. field windings in series and in parallel
    b. field winding in series, armature in parallel
    c. armature in series, field winding in series

26. What is the downside to series generators?
    a. difficult to troubleshoot
    b. poor voltage regulation
    c. they require a field rheostat
    d. the "coming in" speed is higher than that of parallel or compound

27. How is the voltage in a shunt generator controlled?
    a. rheostat
    b. capacitor
    c. resistor
    d. rectifier

28. What is/are the advantage(s) of a starter-generator?
    a. saves space and weight
    b. easier to start engine
    c. unit is simplistic in design

29. Modern GCUs for high output generators use what type of electronic circuits to sense operations?
    a. loop circuits
    b. open circuits
    c. closed circuits
    d. solid state circuits

30. What voltage sensitive device is found in almost all voltage regulating circuitry?
    a. zener diode
    b. excitation relay
    c. solenoid

31. What is/are the benefit(s) of DC alternators over DC generators?
    a. lighter, more reliable
    b. lighter, more efficient
    c. less space, easier maintenance
    d. easier maintenance

32. How many wire coils does a typical DC alternator have?
    a. 1
    b. 2
    c. 3
    d. 4

33. Why are ACU's considered more reliable than vibrating-type regulators?
    a. no moving parts
    b. do not require transistor circuitry to control current
    c. provide addition protection like over- and under- current protection
    d. more simplistic

34. Which of the following is the proper symbol for a diode?
    a.
    b.
    c.
    d.

35. How do zener diodes and regular diodes differ?
    a. zener diodes can withstand higher voltage values
    b. regular diodes have a breakdown value
    c. zener diodes permit reverse current flow over a certain voltage
    d. zener diodes permit reverse current flow over a certain current

36. The exciter generator in an AC alternator contains which of the following?
    a. armature and permanent magnet
    b. armature and field winding
    c. armature and field windings

37. What is the frequency of an AC alternator?
    a. 400 Hz ± 5%
    b. 400 Hz ± 10%
    c. 400 Hz ± 15%
    d. 400 Hz ± 20%

38. How does the speed control unit of a CSD adjust the hydraulic pressure to control output speed?
    a. piston pump
    b. wobble plate
    c. gear reduction
    d. valve assembly

39. Why are starter motors controlled through a solenoid?
    a. to prevent damage in case of starter malfunction
    b. to prevent a reverse polarity connection
    c. high voltage draw required for start
    d. high amperage draw required for start

40. What is one of the most important pieces of information when analyzing/troubleshooting the landing gear via the electrical diagrams?
    a. knowing the current value for each segment of the circuit
    b. knowing the different circuits and how they relate to one another
    c. knowing the gear position to ensure correct operation
    d. determining whether there is a short or an open in the circuit

41. What is an LRU?
    a. line replacement unit
    b. line reverser unit
    c. line redundant unit
    d. line resistor unit

42. (Refer to figure 1) When the "gear up" switches are in the *not up* position where does current flow through?
    a. though terminal 2, the squat switch, and the down solenoid
    b. through terminal 1, the squat switch, and the up solenoid
    c. through terminal 3 to the up motor
    d. through terminal 2, the squat switch, and the up solenoid

43. (Refer to figure 1) What happens when the squat switch is activated (ground) and the gear switch is in the up position?
    a. the gear will not retract
    b. the gear will not retract and a warning horn will sound
    c. the gear will retract

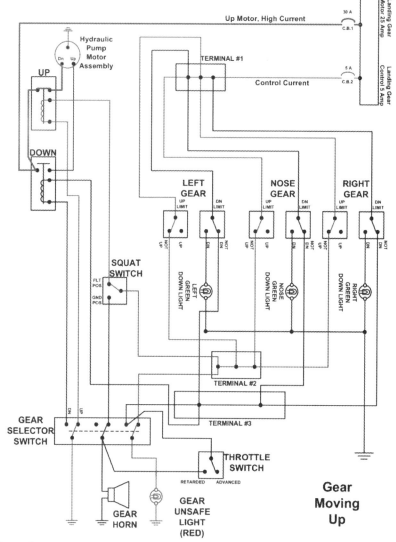

Figure 1

44. (Refer to figure 2) What contacts must be closed for the APU gen to power AC bus 1?
    a. APB, GB2
    b. APB, GB1
    c. APB, BTB1
    d. APB, BTB2

45. (Refer to figure 2) In the event that all generators fail, AC is available through which of the following?
    a. AC ESS INV
    b. AC ESS
    c. STAT INV
    d. ESS TR

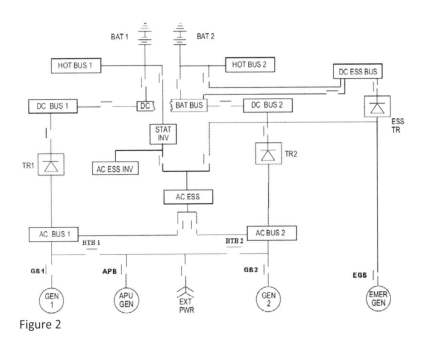

Figure 2

46. What determines the size of an aluminum conductor wire?
    a. current rating
    b. contact current rating
    c. brackets used to hold the wire in place
    d. termination hardware rating

47. What is the maximum deflection between support points of wire bundles?
    a. ¼"
    b. ½"
    c. ¾"
    d. 1"

48. What is static bonding?
    a. low-impedance paths to the aircrafts structure for electrical equipment
    b. conductive objects on the exterior of the airframe electrically connected through mechanical joints to the airframe
    c. conductive parts subject to electrostatic charging mechanically secured through an electrical connection to the aircraft structure

49. Which type of switch is spring loaded?
    a. rotary
    b. toggle
    c. micro
    d. rocker

50. (Refer to figure 3) What bus powers the ESS AC BUS during normal operation?
    a. Gen 1
    b. Gen 2
    c. Gen 3
    d. APU Gen

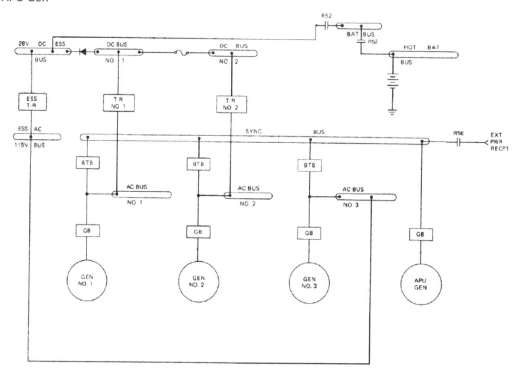

Figure 3

Chapter 10
Aircraft Instruments

Chapter 10 - Section A
Study Aid Questions

Fill in the Blanks

1. There are usually two parts to any instrument or instrument system. One part _____ the

   situation and another part to _____ it.

2. Original analogue flight instruments are operated by _____ pressure and the use of

   _____.

3. 3 fundamental pressure-sensing mechanisms used in aircraft instrument are the _____,

   the _____, and the _____ sensing device.

4. Modern high performance aircraft use a digital air data computer that converts _____

   into _____.

5. ADCs receive input from the _____ sensing devices and process them for use by

   numerous _____.

6. Altimeters that measure an aircraft's _____ by measuring _____

   of the atmosphere are known as _____ altimeters.

7. Digital flight instruments perform all of the calculations for _____
   in the ADC.

8. Many high performance aircraft are equipped with _____ for monitoring Mcrit.

9. A _____ is an electric system used for transmitting information from one point to another.

10. Autosyn systems are distinguished from Magnasyn systems by the fact that the transmitter and indicator rotors used are _____ magnets rather than _____ magnets.

11. The tachometer indicates the speed of the _____ of a reciprocating engine.

12. Some turbine engines use _____ for rpm indication, rather than _____ system.

13. An accelerometer is used to monitor _____ acting upon an airframe and are used in _____ navigation systems.

14. Modern aircraft AOA sensors units send output signals to the _____.

15. Solid state magnetometers can not only sense the _____ to the earth magnetic poles, but also the _____ of the flux field.

16. Gyro instruments are driven by: _____, _____ or _____

17. The attitude indicator, or _____, provides _____ and _____ information.

18. Automatic pilot systems are capable of keeping aircraft stabilized _____, _____, and _____.

19. The four basic components of an autopilot system are:

_____   _____

_____   _____

20. The Electronic Attitude Director Indicator (EADI) is an advanced version of _____

and _____ indicators.

21. The _____ system automatically monitors the airframe and engine systems and alerts the flight crew in case of a system failure.

22. The highest level of automated flight system is the _____.

23. The FMS coordinates the adjustment of _____, _____,

and _____ parameters either automatically or by instructing the pilot how to do so.

24. When an aircraft is to be operational under IFR, an altimeter test must have been performed within the

previous _____ months.

25. Compass magnetic deviation is caused by _____ interference from ferrous

materials and operating _____ components in the cockpit.

TRUE or FALSE

_____ 1. Direct sensing instruments sense and display the information all in one instrument.

_____ 2. The three basic kinds of instruments are classified as: flight instruments, engine instruments, and environmental control instruments.

_____ 3. In a Bourdon tube the higher the pressure of the fluid, the more the tube straightens. True/false

_____ 4. Many flight instruments use a Bourdon type of sensing device.

_____ 5. Solid state pressure sensing systems are internal sensing systems.

_____ 6. The engine pressure indicator (EPR) compares the total exhaust pressure to the pressure of the ram air at the inlet of the engine.

_____ 7. True airspeed is the relationship between the ram air pressure and static air pressure.

_____ 8. The calculations of calibrated airspeed for modern aircraft with digital instruments are performed by the ADC.

_____ 9. Aircraft with direct current systems (DC) often use synchro systems for transmitting information from one point to another.

_____ 10. Tachometers used for turbine engines monitor the speed of the compressor section of the engine.

_____ 11. Two types of Angle of Attack sensors used in aircraft are the vane type which uses an alpha vane externally mounted to the outside of the fuselage and the other type uses two slots in a probe that extends out of the side of the fuselage.

_____ 12. Some AOA systems incorporate a stick pusher actuator that pushes the control yoke backwards to lower the nose of the aircraft.

_____ 13. Two common application of thermocouples are: cylinder head temperature in reciprocating engines and exhaust gas temperature in turbine engines.

_____ 14. Total air temperature (TAT) is the static air temperature minus any lowering in temperature caused by flying at high altitudes.

_____ 15. Magnetic deviation, variation and dip errors are errors associated with a magnetic compass?

_____ 16. The process for knowing how to adjust for magnetic variation is known as swinging the compass.

_____ 17. Ring Laser Gyros (RLG), Microelectromechanical systems and Attitude Heading and Reference Systems (AHRS) are examples of attitude and directional systems used on modern aircraft.

_____ 18. The sensing elements of an autopilot system are: the attitude and directional gyros, the turn coordinator, magnetic compass, and an altitude control.

_____ 19. The output elements of an autopilot system are the servos that cause actuation of the flight control surfaces.

_____ 20. The electronic flight instrument system replaces the attitude indicator and vertical gyro by cathode ray tubes (CRT) or LCDs that display EADI and EHSI presentations.

_____ 21. The EICAS monitors engine and airframe parameters and doesn't utilize traditional gauges.

_____ 22. Maintenance personnel can access the EICAS to access data related to a failure event.

_____ 23. The master caution lights on the enunciator panel can not be cancelled by the flight crew.

_____ 24. Instrument panels are usually shock mounted to absorb high frequency, high-amplitude shocks.

_____ 25. The original equipment manufacturer will put colored range markings on the instrument face in accordance with the type certificate data sheet.

---

1. What is used as a reference for range marking instruments?

2. What does a yellow arc on an instrument dial indicate?

3. What aircraft instrument may be used to check a manifold pressure indicator for correct indication?

4. What indication errors may be found in altimeters?

5. What flight instruments are usually connected to a pitot-static system?

6. What is required after replacement of components connected to a pitot-static system?

7. What methods are used to drive turn-and-bank indicators?

8. What is a synchro-type remote indicating system?

9. What does a tachometer indicate?

10   What type of indicating system is used to measure the turbine-engine exhaust gas temperature?

11   What is the meaning of swinging a compass?

12   Name the three types of basic instruments used in an aircraft flight station?

13   What does an engine pressure indicator (EPR) compare?

14. What equipment performs the calculation of calibrated airspeed for modern aircraft with digital instruments?

15   Describe the two types of Angle of Attack sensors used in aircraft.

16. What are the two most common applications of thermocouples?

17. What type of system does monitor engine and airframe parameters and does not utilize traditional gauges.

18. What system can be accessed by maintenance personnel to access data related to a failure event.

19. What type of instrument maintenance can be performed by certificated A & P mechanics?

20. Name at three systems or components that provide input to the flight management computer (FMC)?

1. Aircraft instrument panels are generally shock mounted to absorb:
   a. all vibration
   b. low frequency, high amplitude shocks
   c. high frequency, high amplitude shocks

2. Aircraft instruments should be marked and graduated in accordance with:
   a. the instrument manufacturer's specifications
   b. both the aircraft and engine manufacturers' specifications
   C) the specific aircraft maintenance or flight manual

3. What marking color is used to indicate if a cover glass has slipped?
   a. red
   b. white
   c. yellow

4. The green arc on an aircraft temperature gauge indicates:
   a. the instrument is not calibrated
   b. the desirable temperature range
   c. a low, unsafe temperature range

5. Which instruments are connected to an aircraft's pitot static system?
   1. Vertical speed indicator.   *2. Cabin altimeter.*   *3. Altimeter.*
   4. Cabin rate-of-change indicator.   *5. Airspeed indicator.*
   a. 1, 2, 3, 4, and 5.
   b. 1, 2, and 4.
   c. 1, 3, and 5.

6. An aircraft instrument panel is electrically bonded to the aircraft structure to:
   a. act as a restraint strap.
   b. provide current return paths.
   c. aid in the panel installation.

7   A radar altimeter indicates
   a. flight level (pressure) altitude.
   b. altitude above sea level.
   c. altitude above ground level.

8   When installing an instrument in an aircraft, who is responsible for making sure it is properly marked?
   a. The aircraft owner.
   b. The instrument installer.
   c. The instrument manufacturer.

9. Where may a person look for the information necessary to determine the required markings on an engine instrument?

        1. Engine manufacturer's specifications.   *2. Aircraft flight manual.*
        3. Instrument manufacturer's specifications.   *4. Aircraft maintenance manual.*

    a. 2 or 4
    b. 1 or 4
    c. 2 or 3

10. A certificated mechanic with airframe and powerplant ratings may:
    a. perform minor repairs to aircraft instruments
    b. perform minor repairs and minor alterations to aircraft instruments
    c. not perform repairs to aircraft instruments

11. Which instruments are connected to an aircraft's static pressure system only?

        1. Vertical speed indicator   *2. Cabin altimeter*   *3. Altimeter*
        4. Cabin rate-of-change indicator   *5. Airspeed indicator*

    a. 1 and 3
    b. 2, 4, and 5
    c. 2 and 4

12. If a static pressure system check reveals excessive leakage, the leak(s) may be located by
    a. pressurizing the system and adding leak detection dye
    b. isolating portions of the line and testing each portion systematically, starting at the instrument connections
    c. removing and visually inspecting the line segments

13. Which of the following instrument discrepancies would require replacement of the instrument?

        1. Red line missing   *2. Case leaking*   *3. Glass cracked*
        4. Mounting screws loose   *5. Case paint chipped* *6. Leaking at line B nut*
        7. Will not zero out   *8. Fogged*

    a. 2, 3, 7, 8
    b. 1, 4, 6, 7
    c. 1, 3, 5, 8

14. The red radial lines on the face of an engine oil pressure gauge indicates:
    a. minimum engine safe RPM operating range.
    b. minimum precautionary safe operating range.
    c. minimum and/ or maximum safe operating limits.

15. A Bourdon tube instrument may be used to indicate

        1. pressure   *2. temperature*   *3. position*

    a. 1 and 2
    b. 1
    c. 2 and 3

16. An aircraft magnetic compass is swung to up-date the compass correction card when :
    a. an annual inspection is accomplished on the aircraft
    b. the compass is serviced
    c. equipment is added that could effect compass deviation

17. When swinging a magnetic compass, the compensators are adjusted to correct for:
    a. magnetic influence deviation
    b. compass card oscillations
    c. magnetic variations

18. The maximum altitude loss permitted during an unpressurized aircraft instrument static pressure system integrity check is:
    a. 50 feet in 1 minute
    b. 200 feet in 1 minute
    c. 100 feet in 1 minute

19. A barometric altimeter indicates pressure altitude when the barometric scale is set at:
    a. 29.92 inches Hg
    b. 14.7 inches Hg
    c. field elevation

20. The function of a CRT in an EFIS is to:
    a. allow the pilot to select the appropriate system configuration for the current flight situation.
    b. display alphanumeric data and representations of aircraft instruments.
    c. receive and process input signals from aircraft and engine sensors and send the data to the appropriate display.

21. Who is authorized to repair an aircraft instrument?
    1. A certified mechanic with an airframe rating.
    2. A certificated repairman with an airframe rating.
    3. A certificated repair station approved for that class instrument.
    4. A certificated airframe repair station.
    a. 1, 2, 3, and 4
    b. 3 and 4
    c. 3

22. A synchro transmitter is connected to a synchro receiver:
    a. mechanically through linkage.
    b. electromagnetically without wires.
    c. electrically with wires.

23. A turn coordinator instrument indicates:
    a. the longitudinal attitude of the aircraft during climb and descent
    b. both roll and yaw
    c. the need for corrections in pitch and bank

24. What does a reciprocating engine manifold pressure gauge indicate when the engine is not operating?
    a. Zero pressure
    b. The differential between the manifold pressure and the atmospheric pressure
    c. The existing atmospheric pressure

25. The Flight Management System coordinates the adjustment of?
    a. Flight parameters only
    b. Engine parameters only
    c. Engine parameters, flight parameters, airframe parameters

26. The system that automatically monitors the airframe and engine systems and alerts the flight crew in case of a system failure is called?
    a. EADI
    b. AFCS
    c. ECAM

27. An accelerometer is used to monitor _____ acting upon an airframe.
    a. Pressures
    b. Forces
    c. Airflow

28. The engine pressure indicator (EPR) compares
    a. The total exhaust pressure to the pressure of the ram air at the inlet of the engine.
    b. The total manifold pressure to the pressure at the inlet of the engine.
    c. The total turbine pressure to the pressure of the ram air at the inlet of the engine

29. Thermocouples are used to monitor?
    a. Cylinder head temperature
    b. Exhaust gas temperature in turbine engines
    c. Both A and B

30. What system can be accessed by maintenance personnel to access data related to a failure event.
    a. ADC
    b. EICAS
    c. EFIS

Chapter 11
Communication / Navigation

Chapter 11 - Section A
Study Aid Questions

Fill in the Blanks

1. Covalent bonds are created when two or more substances share electrons in their _____.

2. Electron flow occurs when there are _____ in the valence shell due to the atom's preference

   to have _____ electrons in all of its shell.

3. A four-layer diode or _____ has three junctions. The behavior of the junctions can be

   understood by considering it to be two interconnected _____ transistors.

4. SCRs are often used in high _____ situations, such as switching, phase controls, battery

   chargers, and _____ circuits.

5. The _____ and amount of voltage applied to the gate can widen and narrow the

   _____ due to expansion or shrinkage of the depletion area at the junction of the
   semiconductor.

6. Depletion mode MOSFETs are considered normally _____ while enhanced mode MOSFETZs

   are normally _____.

7. Forward biased _____ give off energy visible in the _____ characteristic
   unique to the material of the semiconductor being used.

8. Transistors are rated by the _____ of the collector current to the _____ current, or Beta.

9. Common-_____ amplifiers are unique because their construction creates a situation where

   the base current is _____ than the collector or emitter current.

10. If there is to be an output voltage in a _____ gate, then the inputs cannot both have voltage.

11. The primary flight display displays the attitude indicator in the _____ half of the display

   and the electronic _____ indicator on the other half.

12. The electronic field component and the electromagnetic field component are oriented _____ to

   each other and at _____ to the direction that the wave is traveling.

13. 2 common methods of modulating _____ waves are amplitude and _____ modulation.

14. FM is considered _____ to AM for carrying and deciphering information on

   _____ waves.

15. The information signal is separated from the carrier wave portion of the signal by the _____

   _____

16. Antennas are _____. They radiate and receive waves in certain patterns and

   _____.

17. _____ wire is used to connect transmitters and receivers to their _____.

18. VORs are marked on aeronautical charts along with their name, the _____ to tune,

   and a _____ designator.

19. On an RDF system, the only way to determine if the aircraft was flying to or from the _____

was the increasing and decreasing strength of the _____ signal.

20. The combination of a magnetic compass, VOR, and ADF into one instrument is found on an _____.

21. Vertical guidance required for an aircraft to descend for landing is provided by the _____

at an angle of about _____.

22. A _____ transponder provides positive identification and _____
of an aircraft on the radar screen of ATC.

23. Traffic collision _____ systems, or TCAS, are _____based
air-to-air traffic monitoring and alerting systems.

24. The _____ covering the antenna must only be painted with approved paint to
allow radio signals to pass unobstructed.

25. The GPS receiver measure the time it takes for a signal to arrive from _____ transmitting

satellites. This two-dimensional position is expressed in _____ coordinates.

TRUE or FALSE

_____ 1. Maintenance of avionics is typically done by a technician with an Airframe license.

_____ 2. Analog representations are discontinuous.

_____ 3. Diodes act as check valves in AC circuits.

_____ 4. Tetrodes are used at higher frequencies than triodes.

_____ 5. Semiconductors are thought to be the building blocks of modern electronics.

_____ 6. A material is an insulator if the electrons in the valence shell are allowed to move freely from one shell
to another.

_____ 7. N-type semiconductor material is also known as a donor material.

_____ 8. The amount of current that is allowed to pass through a forward biased diode is indirectly
proportional to the amount of voltage applied.

_____ 9. A transistor is a sandwich of N-type material between two pieces of P-type material and vice versa.

_____ 10. Current to the collector-emitter is turned on and off by the voltage applied to the collector.

_____ 11. Photodiodes can carry more current than a photon activated transistor.

_____ 12. Rectifiers change AC voltage to DC voltage.

_____ 13. Common-emitter circuits are characterized by high power gains.

_____ 14. A sine wave is produced by generators when an conductor is rotated in a uniform electric field.

_____ 15. Digital logic is based on the binary numbering system.

_____ 16. All gates are amplifiers subject to output fluctuations.

_____ 17. The negative OR gate is the same as the NOR gate.

_____ 18. The relationship between frequency and wavelength is directly proportional.

_____ 19. Ground waves are useful for long distance transmissions.

_____ 20. VHF communication radios range from 118.0MHz to 336.975MHz.

_____ 21. The distance a carrier wave travels is directly related to the amplification of the signal sent to the antenna.

_____ 22. Most radio transmitters generate an unstable oscillating frequency that is stabilized by a mixer.

_____ 23. A transceiver is a communication radio that transmits and receives.

_____ 24. The strongest signals received align directly with the length of the antenna.

_____ 25. The course deviation indicator on an OBS is essentially vertical but moves right and left across graduations each representing 5° of course deviation.

_____ 26. The VOR circuitry is still active on an VOR/ILS receiver when the ILS localizer frequency is tuned in.

_____ 27. DME distances are slant distances which is longer than ground distance.

_____ 28. Transponder code 7700 is used for hijack situations.

_____ 29. A radio altimeter indicates altitude in MSL.

_____ 30. The accuracy of GPS is within 20 meters horizontally and can be improved to 7.6 meters with the integration of WAAS to the GPS.

1. How are analog electric signals modified?

2. Why were vacuum tubes replaced by solid-state devices in aircraft radios?

3. Why is silicon one of the primary materials used in the manufacturing of semi-conductors?

4. When is a semi-conductor said to be reversed biased and what is the resulting effect of the circuit?

5. What does it mean when a diode is designed with a zener voltage and why are they used?

6. What are the advantages of a UJT over a bipolar transistor?

7. What are Shockley diodes useful for?

8. What are the three basic amplifier types?

9. Explain what a NOT gate does in terms of Logic in and out and what this means in relation to voltage.

10. What is the difference between an EXCLUSIVE OR and an OR?

11. Explain the processes of transmitting radio waves.

12. What is demodulation in amplitude modulation?

13. Why is frequency modulation considered superior to amplitude modulation?

14. What are the three frequencies produced when two AC signals are mixed together?

15. What is the purpose of the receiver and what does it do?

16. What are the three characteristics of concern when considering an antenna?

17. How is the use of one-quarter of the wavelength antenna possible?

18. What is antenna field directivity?

19. Describe the difference between dipole, Marconi, and loop antennas.

20. How does a VOR receiver interpret the signal generated by the VOR station?

21. Describe each of the radio transmissions used on an ILS approach.

22. What does pressing IDENT do for an ATC controller?

23. When is TCAS II required and what does it provide?

24. What are the advantages of ADS-B over conventional ground-based radar?

25. What are the three segments of GPS?

1. As of 1994, how many satellites currently make up the global positioning system?
    a. 15
    b. 24
    c. 31

2. Which of the follow is an advantage of digital electronics over analog electronics?
    a. Continuously voltage modification
    b. Easily modified by small inputs
    c. Better noise control

3. What happens to electrons when they are heated?
    a. Expand their orbit
    b. Contract their orbit
    c. Nothing

4. What does a triode contain that a diode does not?
    a. Heater
    b. Grid
    c. Screen grid

5. How is the screen grid powered?
    a. Positive DC voltage
    b. Positive AC voltage
    c. Negative AC voltage

6. A negatively doped semi-conductor is bonded to what type of element?
    a. An element with 5 valence electrons
    b. An element with 3 valence electrons
    c. An element with 4 valence electrons

7. The ease with which electron movement occurs at a give voltage is affected by which of the following?
    a. Heat
    b. Polarity
    c. Conductivity of material

8. Current does not flow through a transistor unless
    a. Voltage is applied to the base, narrowing the depletion area at the base-emitter
    b. Voltage is applied to the collector, narrowing the depletion area at the collector-base
    c. Voltage is applied to the emitter, widening the depletion area at the base-emitter

9. Which of the following is a characteristic of an SCR?
    a. has a zener voltage
    b. Has a break over voltage rather than a breakdown voltage
    c. Limit current flow to one direction

10. A unijunction transistor does not have which of the following?
    a. Base material
    b. Collector material
    c. Emitter material

11. Channel is a material found in which of the following?
    a. UJT
    b. SCR
    c. FET

12. A three-phase AC circuit is rectified with a:
    a. 3 diode circuit
    b. 4 diode circuit
    c. 6 diode circuit

13. Common-collector circuits are characterized by
    a. High current gain and 180° voltage phase shift from input to output
    b. High current gain but practically no voltage gain
    c. Attenuates current but causes a high gain in voltage

14. A tank circuit is one with:
    a. A capacitor and coil in parallel with one another
    b. A capacitor and coil in series with one another
    c. A capacitor and resistor in parallel with one another

15. The output of a negative AND gate is the same as a(n):
    a. EXCLUSIVE OR
    b. NAND
    c. NOR

16. Which of the following is a consolidation of various communication and navigation controls?
    a. Audio panel
    b. Digital tuner
    c. Both A & B

17. What are the frequency ranges and names given to VLF, LF, and MF waves?
    a. 3kHZ-3mHZ, ground waves
    b. 2MHz-25MHz, surface waves
    c. 3kHz-30mHz, sky waves

18. Which of the following frequencies contain the information signal after it comes out of the mixer?
    a. Radio frequency
    b. Local oscillator frequency
    c. Difference frequency

19. How can radio antennas be made effectively shorter?
    a. Adding a properly rated capacitor in series with the transmission line
    b. Adding an inducer in the circuit
    c. Both A & B

20. For optimum performance, the impedance of the transmission line should be equal to the impedance of the antenna, which is often
    a. 5 ohms
    b. 50 ohms
    c. 75 ohms

21. When is the reference signal of a VOR in phase with the variable signal?
    a. Magnetic north
    b. 90°
    c. 180°

22. Where are VOR receivers operationally tested and what is the maximum acceptable error?
    a. VOT, ±2°
    b. Avionics repair station, ±4°
    c. VOT, ±4°

23. NDB signals are modulated with what unique identifying characteristic?
    a. Aural identifiers
    b. Morse cold pulses
    c. Both A & B

24. Which of the following lights represents a marker beacon signal?
    a. Blue
    b. Amber
    c. White

25. Altitude encoders provide what addition information to a radar beacon transponder?
    a. Pressure altitude
    b. Density altitude
    c. Neither A or B

26. According to Title 14 CFR 91 section 91.413, all transponders on aircraft flown in controlled airspace are required to be inspected and tested every
    a. 30 days
    b. 12 calendar months
    c. 24 calendar months

27. Magenta is reserved for which of the following on on-board weather radar receivers?
    a. Heavy precipitation
    b. Extreme precipitation
    c. Wind shear

28. Which of the following provides an actual return on weather radar?
    a. Severe turbulence
    b. Wind shear
    c. Hail

29. How are ELTs activated?
    a. Manually by pilot in an accident
    b. As a result of excessive G-forces
    c. Either A or B

30. How are separation minimums reduced for precision approaches?
    a. GPS equipped aircraft
    b. WAAS equipped aircraft
    c. IRS equipped aircraft

Chapter 12
Hydraulic Systems

Chapter 12 - Section A
Study Aid Questions

Fill in the Blanks

1. Hydraulic operations are roughly _____ % efficient, with _____ loss due to fluid friction.

2. The 3 principle categories of hydraulic fluids are: _____, _____, and _____base.

3. Phosphate ester based fluids are used mostly in transport category aircraft which is commonly referred to as

   _____. Presently, type _____ and _____ are used exclusively.

4. Hydraulic systems require special accessories such as _____, _____, and _____ to be compatible with the fluid being used.

5. Filter ratings are given in terms of _____, and is an indication of the _____ size that will be filtered out.

6. Differential pressure indicators are designed to prevent false indications due to _____,

   _____, or _____.

7. Power packs are driven by either a(n) _____ or _____.

8. Reservoirs can be pressurized or _____. Commercial transport aircraft have

   pressurized reservoirs and most of them use _____ to do this.

9. A filter is a(n) _____ or _____ device used to

clean the hydraulic fluid, thus _____ foreign contaminates from remaining in the system.

10. Maintenance of filters is relatively easy. It consists mostly of _____ the filter and

element or cleaning the filter and _____ the element.

11. _____ pressure provides a convenient means of monitoring the condition

of installed filter elements. It is the _____ used in the differential-pressure or

_____-filter indicators found on many filter assemblies.

12. Once extended, the differential pressure indicator must be _____ and

provides a _____ warning of a loaded element.

13. All aircraft hydraulic systems have one or more _____ pumps and may have a(n)

_____ pump as an additional unit when the _____ pump is inoperative.

14. Pumps may be classified in 1 of 2 categories: _____ or _____ displacement.

15. The _____ section of the drive coupling, located _____ of

the two sets of splines, is _____ in diameter than the splines.

16. Most valves are _____ controlled by a(n) _____ and are sometimes

called _____valves.

17. A sequence valve _____ fluid to a second actuator or motor after a set

_____ has been reached, to do work in another part of the system.

18. A(n) _____ valve will give precedence to the critical hydraulic sub systems over

_____ systems when system pressure is _____.

19. Fuses detect sudden increase in flow such as a(n) _____ downstream, which in turn,

_____ hydraulic fluid for the rest of the system.

20. Pressure relief valves are necessary to prevent _____ of components or _____

of hydraulic lines under _____ pressure.

21. _____ relief valves are used to relieve excessive pressure that may exist due to

_____ of the fluid.

22. Pressure _____ are devices used to manage the output of the _____ to
maintain system operating pressure within a fixed range.

23. The main purpose of the _____ valve is to isolate the normal system from an alternate or emergency

system. The sliding component of this valve is to _____ either one of the other inlet ports.

24. Shut off valves are used to shut off the flow of fluid to a particular _____ or _____.

25. The initial charge of an operational accumulator is known as _____.

TRUE or FALSE
:

_____ 1. Large transport category aircraft hydraulic systems produce around 500 PSI of pressure.

_____ 2. Both a high flash point and a high fire point are desirable for hydraulic fluids.

_____ 3. The only contaminants that really affect a hydraulic system are abrasive type contaminants (ex. sand, rust, and machining chips)

_____ 4. If the system becomes contaminated, it must to be purged immediately.

_____ 5. Basic hydraulic systems have one of the following: directional valve, check valve, pressure relief valve, or selector valve.

_____ 6. A hydraulic power pack does not require a centralized hydraulic power supply or long hydraulic lines.

_____ 7. Pressurized reservoirs use quantity transmitters to gauge fluid quantity in the system.

_____ 8. The micron element is designed to prevent passage of solids greater than 1 micron in size.

_____ 9. Thermal lockout devices incorporated into some button indicators prevent operation of the indicator below a certain temperature.

_____ 10. Most modern power-driven pumps are variable-delivery, compressor-controlled type.

_____ 11. All aircraft axial-piston pumps have an odd number of pistons (5, 7, 9, etc.).

_____ 12. When the pump outlet pressure of a Vickers variable delivery pump is below 2850 psi, it is held at its maximum angle in relation with the drive shaft centerline by the force of the yoke return spring.

_____ 13. There are two types of in-line check valves: simple-type and orifice-type.

_____ 14. Automatic resetting fuses are designed to allow a certain volume of fluid per minute to pass through.

_____ 15. An accumulator is a steel sphere divided into two chambers by a rubber diaphragm.

name: _____

1. What color is mineral base hydraulic fluid?

2. What could happen when Skydrol spills onto plastic resins, vinyl compositions, lacquers and oil base paints?

3. What feature is built into the drive shaft of a hydraulic pump to prevent engine damage in the event of pump seizure or overload?

4. What maintenance action is required to minimize contamination during replacement of a hydraulic unit?

5. What condition will cause the filter by-pass on a hydraulic filter to open and allow in unfiltered fluid?

6. Name four types of hydraulic pumps?

7. What sources could pressurize a pressurized hydraulic reservoir?

8. What is the purpose of a pressure relief valve?

9. What is the purpose of a pressure regulator?

10. What is used in some hydraulic systems to supplement the power pump output during high demand?

11. What is the purpose of restrictors that are used in aircraft pneumatic systems?

12. Why should a pneumatic system be purged periodically?

13. What must be accomplished with an accumulator prior to disassembling?

14. Can different hydraulic fluid types be mixed? Why?

15. Why do most aircraft hydraulic installations require a closed center hydraulic system?

16. What is the advantage of a powerpack hydraulic system?

17. Why are hydraulic reservoirs of many transport type aircraft pressurized?

18. Explain the principle of operation of a filter by-pass valve.

19. Name 2 examples of non positive displacement pumps.

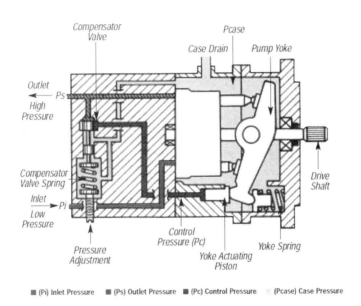

■ (Pi) Inlet Pressure   ■ (Ps) Outlet Pressure   ■ (Pc) Control Pressure   (Pcase) Case Pressure

20. Refer to the figure above. What happens when the control pressure (Pc) increases?

21. Refer to the figure above: What happens when the pressure adjustment screw will be turned clockwise?

22. How are sequence valves controlled?

23. What is the function of the Power transfer unit used in large aircraft hydraulic systems?

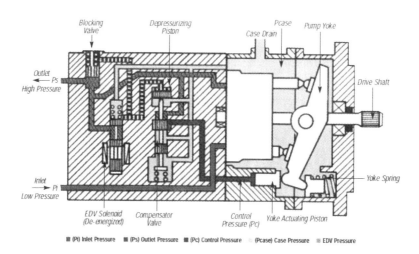

24. Refer to the figure above: What will happen if the EDV solenoid will be energized?

25. What is the reason for using pressure reducing valves?

26. What are the functions of an accumulator?

a]

b]

c]

d]

27. What is the function of the Ram Air Turbine that is often installed in large transport type aircraft?

28. What is pneudraulics?

—

29. Refer to the figure below. What will happen if the fluid level in the reservoir drops below the standpipe?

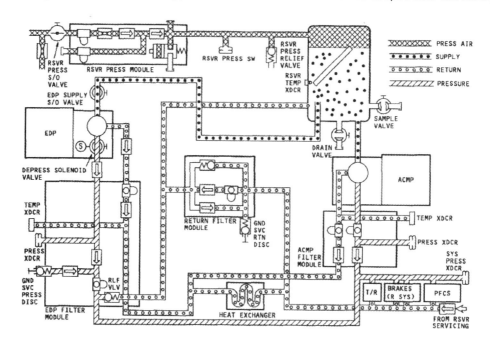

Chapter 12 - Section C
Final Chapter Exam

1. What are the main subsystems of every hydraulic system?
   a. Pump, reservoir, accumulator, heat exchanger, and filtering system
   b. Pump, transfer pump, reservoir, heat exchanger, and filtering system
   c. Pump, carburetor, accumulator, heat exchanger, and filtering system
   d. Pump, reservoir, accumulator, condenser unit, and filtering system

2. Which of the following states that the pressure applied to any part of a confined liquid is transmitted with undiminished intensity to every other part?
   a. Archimedes' principle
   b. Pavlov's Law
   c. Pascal's Law

3. Which of the following are properties should be considered when choosing a fluid for a given hydraulic system.
   a. Viscosity
   b. Chemical stability
   c. Flash point
   d. All of the above

4. Which of the following seals is not compatible with Skydrol?
   a. Neoprene and Buna-N
   b. Butyl rubber and Buna-N
   c. Neoprene and ethylene-propylene
   d. Butyl rubber and ethylene-propylene

5. During maintenance and servicing procedures, all parts should be washed in
   a. Solvent
   b. MEK
   c. Soap and water
   d. Water only

6. Where are filters installed in the system?
   a. Pressure lines
   b. Return lines
   c. Pump case drain lines
   d. All of the above

7. An open center system is one that has fluid flow
   a. unpressurized using a power pump
   b. under pressure using a power pump
   c. and pressure in the system when the actuating mechanism is idle
   d. and no pressure in the system when actuating mechanism is idle

8. If a constant delivery pump is used in a closed system, how is system pressure regulated?
   a. Pump's integral pressure mechanism
   b. Pressure Regulator
   c. Relief Valve

9. What is the advantage of an open system over a closed system?
   a. Continuous pressurization
   b. Faster operation of the system
   c. Gradual pressure buildup
   d. None of the above

10. What is/are the function(s) of a reservoir?
    a. Overflow basin
    b. Purges air bubbles
    c. Heats fluid
    d. A and B are correct

11. How and why are non-pressurized reservoirs kept under a slight pressure?
    a. Bleed air, eliminates foaming and air in the system
    b. Thermal expansion, eliminates foaming and air in the system
    c. Bleed air, ensures positive fluid flow
    d. Thermal expansion, ensures positive fluid flow

12. How are high-altitude aircraft hydraulic system reservoirs pressurized?
    a. Bleed air
    b. Hydraulic pressure pump
    c. Thermal expansion
    d. All of the above

13. A reservoir module consists of which of the following parts?
    a. Filter, sight glass, reservoir bleed valve, reservoir gauge port, temperature transducer
    b. Filter, check valve, test port, manual bleed valve, gauge port
    c. Reservoir pressure relief valve, sight glass, reservoir sample valve, reservoir drain valve, reservoir temperature transducer, reservoir quantity transmitter
    d. Pressure relief valve, manual relief valve, test port, reservoir drain valve, reservoir quantity transducer

14. How can contamination be minimized while adding fluid to the reservoir?
    a. Visually inspect the fluid before pouring it into the system
    b. Use of a Hydraulic filler unit
    c. Pouring hydraulic fluid through a mesh strainer before filling
    d. All of the above

15. Inline filter assemblies are comprised of what three basic units?
    a. Head assembly, bowl, element
    b. Head assembly, module, element
    c. Connecting lines, module, micron filter
    d. Connecting lines, bowl, filter head

16. Which type of filter is designed to be thrown away after removed from the system?
    a. Magnetic type
    b. Porous metal
    c. Micron
    d. None of the above

17. Power driven pumps can be all the following except:
    a. engine-driven
    b. electric motor driven
    c. air driven
    d. mechanically actuated

18. What type of pump has two mesh gears that revolve in a housing driven by an engine or power unit?
    a. gear pump
    b. gerotor pump
    c. piston pump
    d. vane pump

19. What type of pump has two crescent shaped openings?
    a. gear pump
    b. gerotor pump
    c. piston pump
    d. vane pump

20. How is displacement determined by piston pumps?
    I. size of pistons   II. number of pistons   III. stroke length
    a. I & II only
    b. II & III only
    c. I & III only
    d. all of the above

21. How is the pump output changed to accommodate pressure demands in a variable-deliver pump?
    a. pump compensator
    b. internal pressure changes
    c. centrifugal type vanes
    d. off-center rotor

22. What is the purpose of a selector valve?
    a. allows flow in one direction with no or restricted flow in the opposite direction
    b. converts mechanical motion into one requiring greater power
    c. switches fluid flow through an actuator
    d. enables one unit to automatically set another unit into motion

23. What is the purpose of a check valve?
    a. allows flow in one direction with no or restricted flow in the opposite direction
    b. converts mechanical motion into one requiring greater power
    c. switches fluid flow through an actuator
    d. enables one unit to automatically set another unit into motion

24. Which check valve allows for restricted flow in the opposite direction when closed, and how it is accomplished?
    a. simple-type using a ball and spring
    b. orifice-type using a ball and spring
    c. simple-type using a damping valve
    d. orifice-type using a damping valve

25. How is the direction of flow through a check valve determined?
    a. the inlet side has a larger diameter than the outlet side
    b. stamped arrow marked on the housing
    c. the inlet is marked with a capital "I" and the outlet is marked with a capital "O"
    d. the schematic must be referenced to identify direction of fluid flow

26. What is the primary purpose of a hydraulic fuse?
    a. flow sensing device
    b. safety device
    c. backup device
    d. none of the above

27. Why are pressure relief valves not used as pressure regulators in large hydraulic systems?
    a. internal pressure too high, breaks down the internal units of the valve (ball, sleeve, poppet)
    b. designed for electrically driven systems whereas large systems are generally engine driven
    c. heat transferred from the fluid to the packing rings causes deterioration
    d. they are used in large hydraulic systems

28. What is used when a hydraulic system's pressure must be lowered to a specific amount?
    a. pressure reducing valve
    b. pressure relief valve
    c. pressure regulating valve
    d. pressure controlling valve

29. What is/are function(s) of an accumulator?
       I. dampen pressure surges   II. aid the power pump
       III. convert hydraulic energy to mechanical IV. transfers fluid between two hydraulic systems
    a. I & II only
    b. I, II, and III only
    c. III and IV only
    d. IV only

30. What is the purpose of a sequence valve?
    a. allows flow in one direction with no or restricted flow in the opposite direction
    b. converts mechanical motion into one requiring greater power
    c. switches fluid flow through an actuator
    d. enables one unit to automatically set another unit into motion

Chapter 13 - Landing Gear

Chapter 13 - Section A

Study Aid Questions

Fill in the Blanks

1. Name the three basic arrangements of landing gear used in aircraft:

_____   _____

_____

2. Parasite drag caused by landing gear can be reduced by the addition of _____,

   or _____

3. Most single engine aircraft use a non shock absorbing landing gear made from _____,

   _____, or _____.

4. To keep the shock strut and wheels aligned, most shock struts are equipped with _____,

   and _____.

5. Nose gear shock struts have a _____ to keep the gear aligned
   when the aircraft takes off and the shock strut fully extend.

6. The alignment of a main wheel in the vertical plain is called _____.

7. The electric/hydraulic landing gear system found in many Cessna and Piper aircraft is called a

   _____.

8. The _____ lowers the landing gear if the main power system fails.

9. The proper functioning of a landing gear system and components can be checked by performing a

_____. This is also known as _____the gear.

10. Nose wheel vibration is controlled through the use of a _____.

11. The inner wheel halve of a wheel used on a high performance aircraft is likely to have one or more

_____.

12. All aircraft axle nuts must be installed and _____ in accordance with the airframe manufacturer's maintenance procedures.

13. Overheating of the wheel bearings could be caused by a _____ and results

in a _____ tint to the metal surface.

14. Brinelling is caused by _____. It appears as _____ in the bearing cup raceway.

15. Pushing the _____ of the right rudder pedal activates the brake on the _____ main wheel.

16. The _____ transfers the motions of the pistons to the stack of

_____ and _____ to slow the rotation of the wheel.

17. The _____ is the latest iteration of the multiple disc brake.

18. The three brake actuating systems used are _____,

_____ and _____.

19. Power brake systems use the _____ as the source of power to apply the brakes.

20. The auto brake system is used to stop the wheels automatically after _____ this prevents the wheels from rotating when retracted in the wheel wells.

21. The anti-skid system not only detects wheel _____, it also detects when wheel skid

    is _____.

22. Maximum braking efficiency exists when the wheels are decelerating at a maximum rate but are not

    _____.

23. Brake systems with master cylinders may be bled by _____ or _____ bleeding methods.

24. A flat spot on a tire is the result of the tire _____ on the runway surface.

25. Operation on a grooved runway can cause an aircraft tire tread to develop shallow _____ shaped cuts.

TRUE or FALSE

_____ 1. Most aircraft with a tricycle landing gear use differential braking for steering during ground operations.

_____ 2. When more than two wheels are attached to a landing gear strut, the attaching mechanism is known as a bogie.

_____ 3. Landing gear shock struts are filled with air and synthetic turbine engine oil.

_____ 4. During taxi operations the air in the tires and the hydraulic fluid in the shock strut combine to smooth out bumps.

_____ 5. To check the fluid level of most shock struts, the strut needs to be deflated and fully compressed.

_____ 6. Most smaller aircraft use a powerpack gear retraction system while large aircraft use a hydraulic landing gear retraction system.

_____ 7. Sequence valves are often operated mechanically and priority valves control gear component timing via hydraulic volume adjustments.

_____ 8. Some aircraft use a mechanical emergency release system that unlocks the uplocks and the gear will free fall, while others use a pneumatic power system to lower the gear when the main system fails.

_____ 9. Proximity sensors are used for gear position safety switches on many smaller single engine aircraft.

_____ 10. The most common display for the landing gear being up and locked is an illuminated green light.

_____ 11. Aircraft equipped with a hydraulic nose wheel steering system utilize the steering cylinders as shimmy dampers.

_____ 12. Wheels for modern aircraft use a one piece design which provides superior strength and ease of tire installation.

_____ 13. The two pieces of a two piece aircraft wheel are identical and could be used on both the inside as outside of the wheel assembly.

_____ 14. Aircraft technicians should be careful when they approach or remove a tire. The high internal pressure of the tire can create a catastrophic failure that could be lethal to the technician.

_____ 15. In a fixed disk brake system (Cleveland) the brake caliper and linings adjust their position in relationship to the disc.

_____ 16. Dual disc brakes are used on large transport category aircraft that use hydraulic systems to operate the brake systems.

_____ 17. In general small light aircraft use independent brake systems. A master cylinder provides the hydraulic pressure.

_____ 18. The brake accumulator is an emergency source of power for the brake system.

_____ 19. Autobrake systems on large aircraft do not use the anti skid system to control wheel skid.

_____ 20. In order to bleed the power brake system of a large transport category aircraft the hydraulic system needs to be pressurized.

_____ 21. Type III tires are common general aviation tires, Type V tires are high performance tires found on jet aircraft.

_____ 22. Traditional aircraft tires are bias ply tires while modern large aircraft utilize radial tires.

_____ 23. When checking tire pressure wait at least 30 minutes after a typical landing to ensure the tire has cooled to ambient temperature.

_____ 24. Small pieces of rock or debris can be removed with a probing tool or screwdriver while the tire is on the aircraft and inflated.

_____ 25. Under inflation could be evident from excessive wear on the outside of the tire threads.

name: _____

1. What is used to service an air/oil landing gear shock strut?

2. What regular inspection should be made of the exposed portion of a landing gear strut?

3. What is the purpose of main landing gear torque links and arms?

4. What power sources are normally used to retract landing gear systems?

5. What type of nosewheel steering is provided on small aircraft?

6. What unit prevents nosewheel vibration?

7. What is the purpose of power brake debooster cylinders?

8. Name the common types of brake systems used on aircraft?

9. What must be accomplished before inspecting a wheel brake system for hydraulic leaks?

10. What prevents a split wheel from leaking air through the inner and outer mating surfaces, or the wheel assembly?

11. What is the most important maintenance action for safe, long, aircraft tire service?

12. What are the effects of under inflation on tires?

13. When should a landing gear retraction check be accomplished?

14. What is the indication of excessive heating of a wheel bearing?

15. What is the purpose of an anti-skid system?

16. What is the purpose of a wheel fusible plug?

17. What are some methods of bleeding brakes?

18. What methods are used for transmitting the brake pedal movements to a steering control unit in large aircraft?

19. What prevents a nose landing gear from being retracted with the nosewheel out of the center position?

20. What type of material is used for modern brake rotors on transport category aircraft?

name: _____

1. What should be checked when a shock strut bottoms during a landing?
    a. Air pressure
    b. Packing seals for correct installation
    c. Fluid level

2. Overinflated aircraft tires may cause damage to the:
    a. brake linings
    b. wheel hub
    c. wheel flange

3. What is the function of a cam incorporated in a nose gear shock strut?
    a. Provides an internal shimmy damper
    b. Straightens the nosewheel
    c. Provides steering of aircraft during ground operation

4. Debooster cylinders are used in brake systems primarily to:
    a. reduce brake pressure and maintain static pressure
    b. relieve excessive fluid and ensure a positive release
    c. reduce the pressure to the brake and increase the volume of fluid flow

5. The purpose of a relief valve in a brake system is to:
    a. reduce pressure for brake application
    b. prevent the tire from skidding
    c. compensate for thermal expansion

6. A high speed aircraft tire with a sound cord body and bead may be recapped:
    a. a maximum of three times
    b. only by the tire manufacturer
    c. an indefinite number of times

7. The fusible plugs installed in some aircraft wheels will:
    a. indicate tire tread separation
    b. prevent over inflation
    c. melt at a specified elevated temperature

8. Instructions concerning the type of fluid and amount of air pressure to be put in a shock strut are found:
    a. on the airplane data plate
    b. in the aircraft operations limitations
    c. in the aircraft manufacturer's service manual

9. The primary purpose for balancing aircraft wheel assemblies is to:
    a. prevent heavy spots and reduce vibration
    b. distribute the aircraft weight properly
    c. reduce excessive wear and turbulence

10. The pressure source for power brakes is:
    a. the main hydraulic system
    b. the power brake reservoir
    c. a master cylinder

11 What is the purpose of the torque links attached to the cylinder and piston of a landing gear oleo strut?
    a. Limit compression stroke
    b. Hold the strut in place
    c. Maintain correct wheel alignment

12 When an air/oil type of landing gear shock strut is used, the initial shock of landing is cushioned by:
    a. compression of the air charge
    b. the fluid being forced through a metered opening
    c. compression of the fluid

13 The purpose of a sequence valve in a hydraulic retractable landing gear system is to:
    a. prevent heavy landing gear from falling too rapidly upon extension
    b. provide a means of disconnecting the normal source of hydraulic power and connecting the emergency source of power
    c. ensure operation of the landing gear and gear doors in the proper order

14. Which statement is true with respect to an aircraft equipped with hydraulically operated multiple disk type brake assemblies?
    a. There are no minimum or maximum disk clearance checks required due to the use of self compensating cylinder assemblies
    b. Do not set parking brake when brakes are hot
    c. No parking brake provisions are possible for this type of brake assembly

15. Nose gear centering cams are used in many retractable landing gear systems. The primary purpose of the centering device is to:
    a. align the nosewheel prior to touchdown
    b. engage the nosewheel steering
    c. center the nosewheel before it enters the wheel well

16. How long should you wait after a flight before checking tire pressure?
    a. At least 3 hours
    b. At least 2 hours
    c. At least 30 minutes

17. An electric motor used to raise and lower a landing gear would most likely be a
    a. shunt field series wound motor
    b. split field shunt wound motor
    c. split field series wound motor

18. A landing gear position and warning system will provide a warning in the cockpit when the throttle is
    a. retarded and gear is not down and locked
    b. advanced and gear is down and locked
    c. retarded and gear is down and locked

19. Excessive wear in the center of the tread of an aircraft tire is an indication of:
    a. incorrect camber
    b. excessive toe out
    c. over inflation

20. On most aircraft, the oil level of an air and oil shock strut is checked by:
    a. removing the oil filler plug and inserting a gauge
    b. measuring the length of the strut extension with a certain air pressure in the strut
    c. releasing the air and seeing that the oil is to the level of the filler plug

21. How can it be determined that all air has been purged from a master cylinder brake system?
    a. By operating a hydraulic unit and watching the system pressure gauge for smooth, full scale deflection
    b. By noting whether the brake is firm or spongy
    c. By noting the amount of fluid return to the master cylinder upon brake release

22. The best safeguards against heat buildup in aircraft tires are:
    a. proper tire inflation, minimum braking, and ground rolls into the wind
    b. short ground rolls, slow taxi speeds, minimum braking, and proper tire inflation
    c. minimum braking, proper tire inflation, and long ground rolls

23 In brake service work, the term 'bleeding brakes' is the process of:
    a. withdrawing air only from the system
    b. withdrawing fluid from the system for the purpose of removing air that has entered the system
    c. replacing small amounts of fluid in reservoir

24 Aircraft brakes requiring a large volume of fluid to operate the brakes generally:
    a. use independent master cylinder systems
    b. do not use brake system accumulators
    c. use power brake control valves

25. To prevent a very rapid extension of an oleo shock strut after initial compression resulting from landing impact:
    a. various types of valves or orifices are used which restrict the reverse fluid flow
    b. the metering pin gradually reduces the size of the orifice as the shock strut extends
    c. the air is forced through a restricted orifice in the reverse direction

26. The metering pins in oleo shock struts serve to:
    a. lock the struts in the DOWN position
    b. retard the flow of oil as the struts are compressed
    c. meter the proper amount of air in the struts

27. After performing maintenance on an aircraft's landing gear system which may have affected the system's operation, it is usually necessary to:
    a. conduct a flight test
    b. re-inspect the area after the first flight
    c. make an operational check with the aircraft on jacks

28. Why do tire and wheel manufacturers often recommend that the tires on split rim wheels be deflated before removing the wheel from the axle?
   a. to relieve the strain on the wheel retaining nut and axle threads
   b. as a safety precaution in case the bolts that hold the wheel halves together have been damaged or weakened
   c. to remove the static load imposed upon the wheel bearings by the inflated tire

29. Exposure to and/or storage near which of the following is considered harmful to aircraft tires?

| 1. Low humidity | 2. Fuel | 3. Oil | 4. Ozone |
| 5. Helium | 6. Electrical equipment | 7. Hydraulic fluid | 8. Solvents |

   a. 2, 3, 4, 5, 6, 7, 8
   b. 1, 2, 3, 5, 7, 8
   c. 2, 3, 4, 6, 7, 8

30. On all aircraft equipped with retractable landing gear, some means must be provided to:
   a. retract and extend the landing gear if the normal operating mechanism fails
   b. extend the landing gear if the normal operating mechanism fails
   c. prevent the throttle from being reduced below a safe power setting while the landing gear is retracted

Chapter 14 - Fuel Systems

Chapter 14 - Section A
Study Aid Questions

Fill in the Blanks

1. Fuel with low volatility could cause _____,

   _____, and _____ acceleration.

2. Gasoline must truly burn rather than _____ or _____.

3. Vapor lock is a condition in which AVGAS _____ in a fuel line or other component

   between the fuel tank and the _____

4. Carburetor icing is most common at ambient temperatures of _____ but can occur at much

   higher temperatures especially in _____ conditions.

5. Detonation is the rapid, uncontrolled _____ of fuel due to high _____,

   and _____.

6. Turbine engine fuels have _____ volatility and _____ boiling
   points than gasoline.

7. Large transport category aircraft use often three types of fuel tanks. They are:

   _____ _____ _____

8. There are three types of aircraft fuel tanks: They are:

   _____ _____ _____

9. Aircraft fuel tanks have a low area called a _____ that is designed as a place for contaminants and water to settle.

10. Always route a fuel line below any _____.

11. The most common electric motor operated fuel valves are the _____ valve and the

    _____ type valve.

12. A characteristic of solenoid operated fuel valves is that they open and close _____.

13. The boost pump delivers fuel under positive pressure to the _____.

14. Centrifugal fuel boost pumps used in aircraft with reciprocating engines ensure _____

    pressure and are preventing _____.

15. Reciprocating engine aircraft typically use a _____ engine driven fuel pump.

16. Fuel boost pumps on many large aircraft are used for several different fuel sub systems such as a

    _____, and _____ system.

17. Fuel strainers are designed to trap _____ pieces of debris and prevent their

    passage through the _____.

18. _____ filters are commonly used on turbine powered aircraft. This type of filter

    captures extremely fine particles in the range of _____ microns.

19. _____ are used in turbine powered aircraft to prevent the formation of
    ice in the fuel.

20. Modern aircraft use electric fuel quantity indicators which operate with _____ current.

21. Four basic classifications are used to describe aircraft fuel leaks. They are:

_____   _____

_____   _____

22. Heavy seeps are classified as an area of fuel from _____ to _____ in diameter that forms in 30 minutes.

23. When an integral fuel cell needs to be repaired the tank needs to _____

and tested with a _____ to be certain it can be entered safely.

24. Unstrained water can be detected by a _____ appearance to the fuel.

25. Two types of fueling processes are: _____ and _____

TRUE or FALSE

_____ 1. A fuel jettison system is required on aircraft that have a higher take off weight than landing weight.

_____ 2. Turbine fuel has a much lower flash point than AVGAS.

_____ 3. Vapor lock can be caused by excessively hot fuel, low pressure, or excessive turbulence of the fuel traveling through the fuel system.

_____ 4. Detonation could be recognized by a pinging or knocking sound and it causes a lower cylinder head temperature.

_____ 5. AVGAS 100LL could be distinguished from other fuels by its blue color.

_____ 6. Jet B fuel is the most common jet fuel in the United States and it allows engine restarts at high altitude.

_____ 7. Low and mid wing single reciprocating engine aircraft use a gravity fuel system.

_____ 8. large transport type aircraft typically use integral fuel tanks in each of their wing structures to store the fuel.

_____ 9. A fuel transfer system allows fuel to be transferred from one fuel tank to another and a fuel cross feed system allows any engine to draw fuel from any tank.

_____ 10. Aircraft equipped with integral fuel tanks do not have fuel vent systems instead they use fuel jettison systems to vent the fuel tanks.

_____ 11. Motor and solenoid operated valves used in a fuel system use position enunciator lights to indicate valve position in addition to the switch position.

_____ 12. The fuel boost pump delivers fuel under positive pressure to the fuel control.

_____ 13. A centrifugal boost pump is a constant displacement pump.

_____ 14. A sump is typically located in the highest part of the tank so that the water and contaminants can be drained before the flight.

_____ 15. The most common type of fuel heaters for large transport category aircraft are air/fuel heaters and oil/fuel heaters.

_____ 16. The flight crew uses information of the filter by-pass indicating lights and fuel temperature gauge to know when to turn the fuel heaters on or fuel heaters can work automatically

_____ 17. The disadvantage of electronic fuel quantity systems is that they have many moving components.

_____ 18. Many aircraft with capacitance type fuel indicating systems also use a mechanical indication system to cross check fuel quantity indications.

_____ 19. Fuel flow meters in turbine aircraft measure the volume of the fuel consumed by the engine.

_____ 20. A higher fuel flow indication should result in a higher exhaust gas temperature.

_____ 21. When fuel leaks into a confined area the leak must be monitored every flight.

_____ 22. Microorganisms appear as a visible slime that is dark brown, grey, red, or black in color.

_____ 23. The best solution to stop microorganisms to grow in AVGAS is to keep water from accumulating in the fuel.

_____ 24. The type of fuel to be used is placarded near the fill port on over-the-wing systems and at the fueling station on pressure refueled aircraft.

_____ 25. Aircraft fuel boost pumps can be used on some aircraft to defuel the tanks or the pump of the fuel truck can be used to defuel the airplane.

name: _

1. What is the purpose of a fuel dump system incorporated in many transport category aircraft?

2. Name three types of fuel cells.

_____   _____

_____ .

3. What supports the weight of fuel in a bladder-type fuel cell?

4. What is the purpose of a fuel temperature indicator in a turbine-powered aircraft?

5. What is the purpose of a fuel crossfeed system in multiengine aircraft?

6. What 3 positions may be selected on a fuel tank selector valve?

_____   _____   _____

7. What are drip gauges and sight gauges used for?

8. What type of fueling system is used on large transport category aircraft?

9. What are some advantages of single-point pressure fueling?

10. What method may be used to check a fuel tank for leaks after a patch or weld has been performed?

11. What type of fuel system leak will not be visible by evidence of stains or wet spots?

12. Name four types of fuel quantity gauges that are common?

_____   _____

_____   _____

13. Why is an electronic-type fuel quantity gauge more accurate than others?

14. What is the purpose of fuel tank internal baffles?

15. Why should you wait a period of time after fueling before checking fuel sumps?

16. What is the best way to stop microorganisms to grow in jet fuel?

1. Why are integral fuel tanks used in many large aircraft?
   a. To reduce fire hazards
   b. To facilitate servicing
   c. To reduce weight

2. Regarding the below statements:
   > (1) A fuel pressure relief valve is required on an aircraft positive displacement fuel pump.
   > (2) A fuel pressure relief valve is required on an aircraft centrifugal fuel boost pump.

   a. only No. 1 is true
   b. only No. 2 is true
   c. both No. 1 and No. 2 are true

3. Regarding the below statements:
   > (1) A fuel heater can use engine bleed air as a source of heat.
   > (2) A fuel heater can use engine lubricating oil as a source of heat.

   a. only No. 1 is true
   b. both No. 1 and No. 2 are true
   c. neither No. 1 nor No. 2 is true

4. Regarding the below statements:
   > (1) The function of a fuel heater is to protect the engine fuel system from ice formation.
   > (2) An aircraft fuel heater cannot be used to thaw ice in the fuel screen.

   a. only No. 1 is true.
   b. only No. 2 is true
   c. both No. 1 and No. 2 are true

5. Aircraft defueling should be accomplished:
   a. with the aircraft's communication equipment on and in contact with the tower in case of fire.
   b. in a hangar where activities can be controlled.
   c. in the open air for good ventilation.

6. What method is used on turbine powered aircraft to determine when the condition of the fuel is approaching the danger of forming ice crystals?
   a. Fuel pressure warning
   b. Fuel pressure gauge
   c. Fuel temperature indicator

7. In an electronic type fuel quantity indicating system, the tank sensing unit is a:
   a. capacitor
   b. variable resistor
   c. variable inductor

8. To prevent vapor lock in fuel lines at high altitude, some aircraft are equipped with:
   a. vapor separators
   b. direct injection type carburetors
   c. booster pumps

9. If a bladder type fuel tank is to be left empty for an extended period of time, the inside of the tank should be coated with a film of:
   a. engine oil
   b. linseed oil
   c. ethylene glycol

10. Which of the following could result if microbial growth exists in a jet fuel tank and is not corrected?

   1. Interference with fuel flow   *2. Interference with fuel quantity indicators*
   3. Engine seizure   *4. Electrolytic corrosive action in a metal tank*
   5. Lower grade rating of the fuel   *6. Electrolytic corrosive action in a rubber tank*

   a. 1, 2, 4
   b. 2, 3, 5
   c. 1, 5, 6

11. Regarding the below statements:
   (1) If aviation gasoline vaporizes too readily, fuel lines may become filled with vapor and cause increased fuel flow.
   (2) A measure of a gasoline's tendency to vapor lock is obtained from the Reid vapor pressure test.

   a. only No. 2 is true
   b. both No. 1 and No. 2 are true
   c. neither No. 1 nor No. 2 is true

12. Regarding the below statements:
   (1) On a large aircraft pressure refueling system, a pressure refueling receptacle and control panel will permit one person to fuel or defuel any or all fuel tanks of an aircraft.
   (2) Because of the fuel tank area, there are more advantages to a pressure fueling system in light aircraft.

   a. only No. 1 is true
   b. only No. 2 is true
   c. both No. 1 and No. 2 are true

13. A fuel temperature indicator is located in the fuel tanks on some turbine powered airplanes to tell when the fuel may be:
   a. getting cold enough to form hard ice
   b. in danger of forming ice crystals
   c. about to form rime ice

14. What type of fuel booster pump requires a pressure relief valve?
   a. Concentric
   b. Vane
   c. Centrifugal

15. According to Part 23, what minimum required markings must be placed at or near each appropriate fuel filler cover for reciprocating engine-powered airplanes?
    a. The word 'Avgas' and the minimum fuel grade
    b. The word 'Fuel' and usable fuel capacity
    c. The word 'Avgas' and the total fuel capacity

16. Why is it necessary to vent all aircraft fuel tanks?
    a. To ensure a positive head pressure for a submerged boost pump
    b. To exhaust fuel vapors
    c. To limit pressure differential between the tank and atmosphere

16 Flapper valves are used in fuel tanks to:
    a. reduce pressure
    b. prevent a negative pressure
    c. act as check valves

17. What minimum required markings must be placed on or near each appropriate fuel filler cover on utility category aircraft?
    a. The word 'Avgas' and the minimum fuel grade, and the total fuel tank capacity
    b. The word 'Avgas' and the minimum fuel grade for the engines, and the usable fuel tank capacity
    c. The word 'Avgas' and the minimum fuel grade

18. The use of turbine fuels in aircraft has resulted in some problems not normally associated with aviation gasoline. One of these problems is:
    a. increasing viscosity of fuel as fuel temperature lowers at altitude
    b. higher vapor pressure
    c. microbial contaminants

19. What is the recommended practice for cleaning a fuel tank before welding?
    a. Purge the tank with air
    b. Flush the inside of the tank with clean water
    c. Steam clean the tank interior

20. Pressure fueling of aircraft is usually accomplished through:
    a. pressure connections on individual fuel tanks
    b. at least one single point connection
    c. individual fuel tank overwing and/or fuselage access points

21. Aircraft pressure fueling systems instructional procedures are normally placarded on the:
    a. fuel control panel access door
    b. lower wing surface adjacent to the access door
    c. aircraft ground connection point

22. What is the primary purpose of the crossfeed system?
    a. To allow the feeding of any engine from any tank
    b. To allow the feeding of fuel from one tank for defueling
    c. To provide automatic refueling of a tank to any desired level

23. Fuel is moved overboard in most fuel jettison systems by:
    a. boost pumps
    b. gravity
    c. gravity and engine driven fuel pumps

24. The primary purpose of an aircraft's fuel jettison system is to quickly achieve a:
    a. lower landing weight
    b. balanced fuel load
    c. reduced fire hazard

25. Before fueling an aircraft with the pressure fueling method, what important precaution should be observed?
    a. The truck pump pressure must be correct for that refueling system
    b. The truck pump pressure must be adjusted for minimum filter pressure
    c. The aircraft's electrical system must be on to indicate quantity gauge readings

26. A capacitance type fuel quantity indicating system measures fuel in:
    a. pounds
    b. pounds per hour
    c. gallons

27. Why is the capacitance fluid quantity system more accurate in measuring fuel level than a mechanical type?
    a. Only one probe and one indicator are necessary for multiple tank configurations
    b. It measures in gallons and converts to pounds
    c. It measures by weight instead of volume

28. A drip gauge may be used to measure:
    a. the amount of fuel in the tank
    b. system leakage with the system shut down
    c. fuel pump diaphragm leakage

29. Why are jet fuels more susceptible to water contamination than aviation gasoline?
    a. Jet fuel has a higher viscosity than gasoline
    b. Jet fuel is lighter than gasoline; therefore, water is more easily suspended
    c. Condensation is greater because of the higher volatility of jet fuels

30. What method would check for internal leakage of a fuel valve without removing the valve from the aircraft?
    a. Place the valve in the OFF position, drain the strainer bowl, and with boost pump on, watch to see if fuel flows to the strainer bowl
    b. Remove fuel cap(s), turn boost pump(s) on, and watch for bubbling in the tanks
    c. Apply air pressure on the downstream side of the fuel pump and listen for air passing through the valve

Chapter 15
Ice & Rain Control

Chapter 15 - Section A
Study Aid Questions

Fill in the Blanks

1. Under certain atmospheric conditions, ice can build rapidly on _____ and

   _____.

2. On days when there is visible _____ in the air, ice can form on aircraft leading

   edge surfaces at altitudes where _____ start.

3. Rime ice is _____ in weight than clear ice, and its weight is _____

   significance.

4. _____ ice is brittle and more easily removed than _____ ice.

5. Whenever _____ conditions are encountered, the _____

   characteristics of the airplane will _____.

6. The most common systems used to prevent icing on wing leading edges are _____,

   _____, and _____.

7. There are several methods used to provide heated air. These include bleeding hot air from the

   _____, _____, and

   ram air heated by a _____.

8. Modern aircraft use several onboard _____ to control anti-ice and de-ice aircraft systems.

9. _____ anti-icing systems are also often utilized for vertical and horizontal stabilizer anti-ice systems.

10. Chemical anti-icing systems are often called liquid freeze point depressant systems or _____ systems.

11. General aviation (GA) aircraft and turboprop commuter type aircraft often use a _____

_____ to break of the ice after it has formed on the _____ surfaces.

12. Wing de-ice boots are held against the airfoil surfaces by _____ from the

_____ side of the pumps.

13. Deicer tubes are inflated by an _____,

or by air bled from _____.

14. Propellers are de-iced with _____ or

_____ systems.

15. The electrical window heat system prevents _____ and

_____ on the flight deck windows.

16. The windshields are heated by _____ embedded in the glass or by a

_____ that is applied on the inside of the outer windshield ply.

17. Ice can be visibly detected but most modern aircraft have one or more _____ that warn the flight crew of icing conditions.

TRUE or FALSE

_____ 1. Clear ice forms a smooth sheet of solid ice.

_____ 2. Rime ice has a white appearance.

_____ 3. Ice buildup causes destructive vibration, and hampers true instrument readings.

_____ 4. Control surfaces become unbalanced or frozen due to the buildup of ice.

_____ 5. Radio reception is hampered and engine performance is affected due to the buildup of ice.

_____ 6. For the most part, general aviation aircraft equipped to fly in icing conditions use thermal or electric anti-icing systems that are controlled automatically to prevent the formation of ice.

_____ 7. Large transport category aircraft are equipped with advanced deicing boots.

_____ 8. Some modern large aircraft are using electrical thermal anti-icing systems.

_____ 9. A chemical anti-icing is strictly a anti-icing system to prevent the formation of ice and cannot be utilized as a de-icing system.

_____ 10. Air pressure for a pneumatic wings deice system is supplied by the vacuum pump.

_____ 11. Engine driven air pumps are available in a wet and a dry type and used with Turbine engines.

_____ 12. Most general aviation aircraft are equipped with a dry-type of pump.

_____ 13. The deice control valve is normally energized and releases air from the vacuum pump overboard.

_____ 14. Frost deposits can be removed by placing the aircraft in a warm hangar or by using a deicing fluid.

_____ 15. The rain repellant system should not be operated on dry windows because heavy undiluted repellant will restrict window visibility.

MULTIPLE CHOICE

1. Ice buildup increases _____ and reduces _____.
    a. drag and lift
    b. lift and drag
    c. drag and temperature

2. Thermal wing anti-ice systems for business jet and large transport category aircraft will typically use?
    a. ram air from a combustion heater
    b. air from engine exhaust heat exchangers
    c. bleed air from turbine engine compressor
    d. bleed air from turbine engine combustion section

3. What type of valve controls the flow of bleed air from the pneumatic system to the wing anti-ice ducts?
    a. bleed air valve
    b. wing anti-ice valve
    c. cross feed valve

4. What type of circuits in the onboard computer continuously monitors the wing anti-ice system?
    a. build in test circuits (BITE)
    b. wing anti-ice circuits
    c. bleed air circuits
    d. warning circuits

5. Chemical anti-icing systems are used to protect:
    a. wings and stabilizers
    b. windshields
    c. propeller
    d. all of the above

6. A pneumatic de-icing system removes the ice after it has formed on the leading edge surface.
    a. true
    b. false
    c. only in flight
    d. only on the ground

7. Pneumatic de-icing systems (boots) are used on?
    a. general aviation aircraft
    b. transport category aircraft
    c. general aviation and transport category aircraft
    d. helicopters

8. Engine driven pumps are used for?
    a. gyros
    b. pressurization
    c. deicing system
    d. 1 and 2

9. Why is an oil separator necessary in a de-icing outfitted with a wet pump?
    a. to improve lubrication of the pump
    b. to improve vacuum pressure
    c. to remove the oil from the air

10. On modern aircraft the deicer boots are _____ to the leading edge of a wing.
    a. riveted with flush rivets
    b. bolted with rivnuts
    c. bonded with an adhesive

Chapter 15 - Section B
Knowledge Application Questions

1. What are the two types of ice that are encountered during flight?

2. What are the two basic hazards associated with ice or frost forming on aircraft?

3. What could be the result of ice breaking of the wing and entering the engine intake?

4. Name the areas on an aircraft that could be equipped with deicing or anti-icing systems?

5. Name four types of systems that are used to prevent or control ice formation in aircraft?

6. Describe for what type of applications thermal anti-icing systems are used?

7. Why are the left and right wing anti-ice valves operated at the same time?

8. Explain why and how an electric thermal deicing system is made inoperative when the aircraft is on the ground?

9. Explain how a chemical anti-icing system works.

10. Explain how the pneumatic deice system in the figure below works.

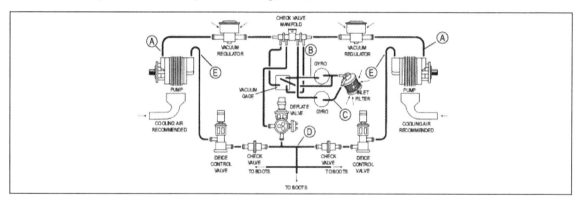

11. Explain why the boot of a pneumatic de-icing system should not stay inflated longer than 7 to 10 seconds?

12. Why do aircraft equipped with turbine engines use bleed air from the engine compressor?

13. What is the reason that dry vacuum pumps do not need any lubricants?

14. What type of rain control systems are used on aircraft?

Final Chapter Exam

1. Arcing in an electrically heated windshield panel usually indicates a breakdown in the:
   a. temperature sensing elements
   b. autotransformers
   c. conductive coating

2. How do deicer boots help remove ice accumulations?
   a. By preventing the formation of ice
   b. By breaking up ice formations
   c. By allowing only a thin layer of ice to build up

3. Why are the tubes in deicer boots alternately inflated?
   a. Alternate inflation of deicer boot tubes keeps disturbance of the airflow to a minimum
   b. Alternate inflation of deicer boot tubes does not disturb airflow
   c. Alternate inflation of deicer boot tubes relieves the load on the air pump

4. Carburetor icing may be eliminated by which of the following methods?
   a. Alcohol spray and heated induction air
   b. Ethylene glycol spray and heated induction air
   c. Electrically heating air intake, ethylene glycol spray, or alcohol spray

5. Why should a chemical rain repellant not be used on a dry windshield?
   a. It will etch the glass
   b. It will restrict visibility
   c. It will cause glass crazing

6. What mixture may be used as a deicing fluid to remove frost from an aircraft surface?
   a. Ethylene glycol and isopropyl alcohol
   b. Methyl ethyl ketone and ethylene glycol
   c. Naphtha and isopropyl alcohol

7. What should be used to melt the ice in a turbine engine if the compressor is immobile because of ice?
   a. Deicing fluid
   b. Anti icing fluid
   c. Hot air

8. What is used as a temperature sensing element in an electrically heated windshield?
   a. Thermocouple
   b. Thermistor
   c. Thermometer

9. What maintains normal windshield temperature control in an electrically heated windshield system?
   a. Thermal overheat switches
   b. Thermistors
   c. Electronic amplifiers

10. What is the principle of a windshield pneumatic rain removal system?
    a. An air blast spreads a liquid rain repellant evenly over the windshield that prevents raindrops from clinging to the glass surface
    b. An air blast forms a barrier that prevents raindrops from striking the windshield surface
    c. A pneumatic rain removal system is simply a mechanical windshield wiper system that is powered by pneumatic system pressure

11. What are three methods of anti icing aircraft windshields?
    1. Blanket type heating system   *2. An electric heating element in the windshield*
    3. Heated air circulating system   *4. Hot water system*
    5. Windshield wipers and anti icing fluid   *6. Ribbon type heating system*
    a. 2, 3, 5
    b. 1, 2, 6
    c. 2, 3, 4

12. What controls the inflation sequence in a pneumatic deicer boot system?
    a. Shuttle valve
    b. Vacuum pump
    c. Distributor valve

13. Which of the following is the best means to use when removing wet snow from an aircraft?
    a. A brush or a squeegee
    b. Hot air
    c. Warm water

14. What is one check for proper operation of a pitot/static tube heater after replacement?
    a. Ammeter reading
    b. Voltmeter reading
    c. Continuity check of system

15. What is the source of pressure for inflating deicer boots on reciprocating engine aircraft?
    a. Vane type pump
    b. Gear type pump
    c. Piston type pump

16. Which of the following regulates the vacuum of the air pump to hold the deicing boots deflated when the pneumatic deicing system is off?
    a. Distributor valve
    b. Pressure regulator
    c. Suction relief valve

17. What may be used to clean deicer boots?
    a. Unleaded gasoline or Jet A fuel
    b. Naphtha
    c. Soap and water

18. Some aircraft are protected against airframe icing by heating the leading edges of the airfoils and intake ducts. When is this type of anti ice system usually operated during flight?
    a. Continuously while the aircraft is in flight
    b. In symmetric cycles during icing conditions to remove ice as it accumulates
    c. Whenever icing conditions are first encountered or expected to occur

19. Which of the following indications occur during a normal operational check of a pneumatic deicer system?
    a. Relatively steady readings on the pressure gauge and fluctuating readings on the vacuum gauge
    b. Fluctuating readings on the pressure gauge and relatively steady readings on the vacuum gauge
    c. Pressure and vacuum gauges will fluctuate as the deicer boots inflate and deflate

20. What method is usually employed to control the temperature of an anti icing system using surface combustion heaters?
    a. Thermo cycling switches
    b. Thermostats in the cockpit
    c. Heater fuel shutoff valves

21. What is the purpose of the distributor valve in a deicing system utilizing deicer boots?
    a. To equalize the air pressure to the left and right wings
    b. To sequence the deicer boots inflations symmetrically
    c. To distribute anti-icing fluid to the deicer boots

22. What is the purpose of the oil separator in the pneumatic deicing system?
    a. To protect the deicer boots from oil deterioration
    b. To remove oil from air exhausted from the deicer boots
    c. To prevent an accumulation of oil in the vacuum system

23. Where are the heat sensors located on most aircraft with electrically heated windshields?
    a. Imbedded in the glass
    b. Attached to the glass
    c. Around the glass

24. Which of the following are found in a laminated integral electrically heated windshield system?
    1. Autotransformer   2. Heat control relay   3. Heat control toggle switch
    4. 24V dc power supply   5. Indicating light

    a. 1, 2, 4, 5
    b. 2, 3, 4, 5
    c. 1, 2, 3, 5

Chapter 16
Cabin Environmental

Chapter 16 - Section A
Study Aid Questions

Fill in the Blanks

1. Oxygen is a _____, _____, and _____
   gas at normal atmospheric temperatures and pressures.

2. The words _____ should be marked clearly on any cylinder
   containing oxygen for aircraft use.
   .

3. Oxygen cylinders are considered empty when the pressure inside drops below _____ psi. This

   ensures that air containing _____ has not entered the cylinder.

4. When oxygen is delivered only as the user inhales, it is known as a _____ system.

5. There are two types of individual oxygen demand regulators: they are:

   _____   _____

6. The main cause of contamination in an oxygen system is _____.

7. The cabin pressurization system must be capable of maintaining a cabin pressure attitude of _____.

   or lower regardless of _____.

8. Metal fatigue from repeated _____, and _____ weakens
   the aircraft structure.

9. There are three typical sources of air used to pressurize reciprocating aircraft. They are:

_____   _____   _____

10. Aircraft equipped with turbine engines typically use _____ as a source for cabin pressurization.

11. Aircraft cabin pressurization systems work in two different modes of operation. They are:

_____   _____

12. The flight crew can select and control _____, _____,

and _____ on the cabin pressure controller.

13. The cabin pressure controller controls the position of the _____ located normally at the rear of the aircraft.

14. Many transport category aircraft have an outflow valve that operates _____ , using

signals sent from a remotely located _____ that act as the pressure regulator.

15. Pressurization safety relieve valves are used to prevent _____ of the cabin.

16. _____ are used to ensure that air pressure outside the aircraft does not exceed cabin air pressure.

17. Aircraft with reciprocating engines often use a _____ cooling system, and turbine

powered aircraft use a _____ cooling system.

18. The air cycle cooling system is supplied with air from either _____ or _____

19. The heart of the air cycle cooling system is the _____, also known as

the _____

20. The duct temperature sensors used in the temperature control system are _____.

Their _____ changes as temperature changes.

21. The temperature at which a substance changes from a _____ into a _____ when heat is added is known as the boiling point.

22. R134a refrigerant is filtered and stored under pressure in a reservoir known as _____

23. Most evaporators are constructed of _____ or _____ tubing coiled into a compact unit.

24. A concern of exhaust shroud heat system is that _____ could contaminate the cabin.

25. Maintenance of combustion heaters consists of routine items such as _____, checking

_____ wear, and ensuring inlets are not plugged.

TRUE or FALSE

_____ 1. Gaseous oxygen systems are used in commercial aircraft and LOX oxygen systems are primarily used in military aircraft.

_____ 2. Most oxygen storage cylinders are painted blue, but yellow and white may be used as well.

_____ 3. Demand-flow systems are used most frequently by the crew on high performance and air transport category aircraft.

_____ 4. A blown out green disk in the side of fuselage indicates that the oxygen supply is low and this should be investigated before flight.

_____ 5. The solid chemical oxygen generators used in most airliners are activated automatically by depressurization or manually by a switch operated by the flight crew.

_____ 6. Petroleum products such as grease and oil should never be used for oxygen system maintenance because an explosion could be the result.

_____ 7. The cabin pressurization system must maintain the cabin pressure altitude below 10,000 ft.

_____ 8. Metal fatigue can result from repeated pressurization cycles and can weaken the airframe structure.

_____ 9. Superchargers are the common source of pressurization on modern reciprocating engine aircraft.

_____ 10. Turbochargers are driven by a shaft or a drive belt.

_____ 11. Large turbine powered aircraft use bleed air from the engine compressor section as a source of air for cabin pressurization.

_____ 12. The isobaric control mode of a cabin pressurization system controls cabin pressure to maintain a constant pressure between the air pressure outside the cabin and the ambient air pressure.

_____ 13. Small aircraft often use a pneumatically controlled outflow valve while transport category aircraft use electrically/electronically controlled outflow valves.

_____ 14. Pressurization safety relieve valves are used to prevent negative cabin pressure.

_____ 15. Many pack valves used in air conditioning systems are electrically controlled and pneumatically operated.

_____ 16. The primary heat exchanger is cooled by an electric fan during stationary ground operations and ram air is used in flight.

_____ 17. The water separator has a fiberglass bag (sock) that condenses and coalesces the mist into larger water droplets. Gravity will drain the water droplets from the water separator.

_____ 18. The function of the refrigeration by-pass valve is to regulate the temperature of the air cycle machine so it does not freeze when passing through the water separator.

_____ 19. A vapor cycle air conditioning system is an open system in which a refrigerant is circulated through tubing and a variety of components.

_____ 20. Most modern vapor cycle cooling systems on aircraft use R12 refrigerant which has replaced the R134a refrigerant.

_____ 21. During a feel test components and lines in the high side (from the compressor to the expansion valve) should warm or hot to the touch.

_____ 22. During a feel test low side lines and the evaporator should be warm.

_____ 23. The charging capacity of a vapor cycle air conditioning system is measured by weight.

_____ 24. Most single-engine light aircraft use a bleed air system to heat the cabin.

_____ 25. The fuel for the combustion heater is drawn from a dedicated small fuel tank inside the cabin.

1. What component in the pressurization system is the principal control of a pressurization system?

2. What source of air supply is used by most turbine-powered aircraft for pressurization?

3. What pressurization control unit will change the position of an outflow valve?

4. On reciprocating engine aircraft, what are some methods of supplying heat to the cabin?

5. What is the function of ventilating air in a combustion heater?

6. What are the typical components used in an air-cycle cooling system?

7. What causes a temperature drop in an air-cycle cooling system?

8. Describe how a water separator in an air cycle cooling system removes moisture from the air?

9. Describe the theory of operation of a vapor-cycle cooling system illustrated in textbook figure 16-74?

10. Describe the theory of operation of an air cycle cooling system illustrated in textbook figure 16-63.

11. What are the main components in a vapor-cycle cooling system?

12. How does a continuous-flow oxygen system operate?

13. What must be accomplished if an oxygen system has been open to atmosphere for 2 hours or more?

14. What is used to purge oxygen lines of moisture?

15. What type of oxygen must be used in aircraft?

16 Why is oil added to a vapor-cycle Freon system?

17. What safety precautions should be observed when servicing oxygen systems?

18. What sources of air are used by pressurized aircraft with a reciprocating engine?

19. What is the main advantage of using LOX systems?

20. What kind of adjustments can be made on a pressure controller?

1. The purpose of the dump valve in a pressurized aircraft is to relieve:
    a. all positive pressure from the cabin
    b. a negative pressure differential
    c. pressure in excess of the maximum differential

2. The basic air cycle cooling system consists of:
    a. a source of compressed air, heat exchangers, and an air cycle machine
    b. heaters, coolers, and compressors
    c. ram air source, compressors, and engine bleeds

3. Frost or ice buildup on a vapor cycle cooling system evaporator would most likely be caused by:
    a. the mixing valve sticking closed
    b. moisture in the evaporator
    c. inadequate airflow through the evaporator

4. In a Freon vapor cycle cooling system, where is cooling air obtained for the condenser?
    a. Turbine engine compressor
    b. Ambient air
    c. Pressurized cabin air

5. What component in a vapor cycle cooling system would most likely be at fault if a system would not take a Freon charge?
    a. Expansion valve
    b. Condenser
    c. Receiver dryer

6. What controls the operation of the cabin pressure regulator?
    a. Cabin altitude
    b. Bleed air pressure
    c. Compression air pressure

7. The cabin pressure of an aircraft in flight is maintained at the selected altitude by
    a. controlling the air inflow rate
    b. inflating door seals and recirculating conditioned cabin air
    c. controlling the rate at which air leaves the cabin

8. What is ventilating air used for on a combustion heater?
    a. Provides combustion air for ground blower
    b. Carries heat to the places where needed
    c. Provides air required to support the flame

9. At which component in an air cycle cooling system does air undergo a pressure and temperature drop?
    a. Expansion turbine
    b. Primary heat exchanger
    c. Refrigeration bypass valve

10. How often should standard weight high pressure oxygen cylinders be hydrostatically tested?
    a. Every 5 years
    b. Every 4 years
    c. Every 3 years

11. Turbine engine air used for air conditioning and pressurization is generally called:
    a. compressed air
    b. ram air
    c. bleed air

12. In an operating vapor cycle cooling system, if the two lines connected to the expansion valve are essentially the same temperature, what does this indicate?
    a. The system is functioning normally
    b. The expansion valve is not metering Freon properly
    c. The compressor is pumping too much refrigerant

13. In the diluter demand oxygen regulator, when does the demand valve operate?
    a. When the diluter control is set at normal
    b. When the user demands 100 percent oxygen
    c. When the user breathes

14. If oxygen bottle pressure is allowed to drop below a specified minimum, it may cause:
    a. the pressure reducer to fail
    b. the automatic altitude control valve to open
    c. moisture to collect in the bottle

15. In a high-pressure oxygen system, if the pressure reducer fails, what prevents high pressure oxygen from entering the system downstream?
    a. Check valve
    b. Pressure relief valve
    c. Manifold control valve

16. What is the condition of the refrigerant as it leaves the condenser of a vapor cycle cooling system?
    a. Low pressure liquid
    b. High pressure liquid
    c. High pressure vapor

17. What is the condition of the refrigerant as it leaves the evaporator of a vapor cycle cooling system?
    a. Low pressure liquid
    b. Low pressure vapor
    c. High pressure vapor

18. The primary difference between aviation breathing oxygen and other types of commercially available compressed oxygen is that:
    a. the other types are usually somewhat less than 99.5 percent pure oxygen
    b. aviation breathing oxygen has had all the water vapor removed
    c. aviation breathing oxygen has a higher percentage of water vapor to help prevent drying of a person's breathing passages and possible dehydration

19. In a gaseous oxygen system, which of the following are vented to blow out plugs in the fuselage skin?
    a. Pressure relief valves
    b. Filler shutoff valves
    c. Pressure reducer valves

20. High pressure cylinders containing oxygen for aviation use can be identified by their:
    a. green color and the words 'BREATHING OXYGEN' stenciled in 1-inch white letters
    b. yellow color and the words 'AVIATOR'S BREATHING OXYGEN' stenciled in 1-inch white letters
    c. green color and the words 'AVIATOR'S BREATHING OXYGEN' stenciled in 1-inch white letters

21. What part of a pressurization system prevents cabin altitude from becoming higher than airplane altitude?
    a. Cabin rate of descent control
    b. Negative pressure relief valve
    c. Positive pressure relief valve

22. The cabin pressure control setting has a direct influence upon the:
    a. outflow valve opening
    b. pneumatic system pressure
    c. inflow valve opening

23. If the cabin rate of climb is too great, the control should be adjusted to cause the:
    a. outflow valve to close slower
    b. outflow valve to close faster
    c. cabin compressor speed to decrease

24. The main cause of contamination in gaseous oxygen systems is:
    a. moisture
    b. dust and other airborne particulates
    c. other atmospheric gases

25. What may be used as a lubricant on oxygen system tapered pipe thread connections?
    a. Silicone dielectric compound
    b. Glycerin
    c. Teflon tape

26. Which is considered a good practice concerning the inspection of heating and exhaust systems of aircraft utilizing a shroud around the engine exhaust as a heat source?
    a. Supplement physical inspections with periodic operational carbon monoxide detection tests.
    b. All exhaust system components should be removed periodically, and their condition determined by the magnetic particle inspection method.
    c. All exhaust system components should be removed and replaced at each 100-hour inspection period.

27. What unit in a vapor cycle cooling system serves as a reservoir for the refrigerant?
    a. Receiver dryer
    b. Evaporator
    c. Condenser

28. Which best describes cabin differential pressure?
    a. Difference between cabin flight altitude pressure and Mean Sea Level pressure
    b. Difference between the ambient and internal air pressure
    c. Difference between cabin pressure controller setting and actual cabin pressure

29. Regarding the statements below:
    (1) Usually bleed air from a gas-turbine engine compressor can be safely used for cabin pressurization.
    (2) Independent cabin condition air machines (air cycle machine) can be powered by
        bleed air from an aircraft turbine engine compressor.

    a. only No. 1 is true
    b. only No. 2 is true
    c. both No. 1 and No. 2 are true

30. The cabin pressurization modes of operation are:
    a. isobaric, differential, and maximum differential
    b. differential, unpressurized, and isobaric
    c. ambient, unpressurized, and isobaric

Chapter 17 - Fire Detection

Chapter 17 - Section A
Study Aid Questions

Fill in the Blanks

1. Because fire is one of the most dangerous threats to an aircraft, the potential fire zones of modern

   multi-engine aircraft are protected by _____ system.

2. 3 detector systems in common use are the _____, _____,

   and _____.

3. A thermocouple depends on the _____ and will not give a warning

   when an engine _____ overheats or a short circuit develops.

4. The thermocouple is constructed of two dissimilar metals such as_____ and

   _____.

5. Two widely used types of continuous-loop systems are _____ type

   detectors such as the Kidde and the Fenwal systems, and the pneumatic pressure detector such as the

   _____ system.

6. The Kidde continuous-loop system can supply _____ data to the airplane
   condition monitoring function of the Aircraft In-flight Monitoring System.

7. Dual loop systems use a _____ logic to increase system reliability.

8. Lindberg systems are also know as _____ and

_____.

9. A smoke detection system monitors the_____, _____, and

    baggage compartments for the presence of _____, which is indicative of fire condition.

10. Optical sensors often referred to as _____.

11. Carbon monoxide detectors are installed in the cockpit of aircraft powered by _____

    engines to detect for _____ gas which can enter the cockpit through

    _____ malfunctions.

12. Class A type fires are best controlled with _____ by cooling the material below its

    _____ temperature and soaking the material to prevent re-ignition.

13. _____ is not recommended for hand-held extinguishers for internal aircraft use.

14. _____ systems use open-end tubes to deliver a quantity

    of extinguishing agent in _____ seconds.

15. Fire extinguisher containers (HRD bottles) store a _____ halogenated extinguishing

    agent and pressurized _____ and are normally manufactured from stainless steel.

TRUE or FALSE

_____ 1. A fire protection system on most aircraft consists of a fire detection and a fire extinguishing system.

_____ 2. Smoke detectors are not used in cargo and baggage compartments.

_____ 3   Class D fires are fires involving energized electrical equipment where the use of an extinguishing
            media that is electrically nonconductive is important.

_____ 4. Thermal switches are pressure-sensitive units that complete electrical circuits at a certain
            temperature.

_____ 5. Transport aircraft almost exclusively use continuous thermal sensing elements for power plant and
            wheel well protection.

_____ 6. Halocarbon clean agents or water are used on a Class D fire.

_____ 7. The Fenwal system uses a slender Inconel tube packed with thermally sensitive eutectic salt and a nickel wire center conductor.

_____ 8. When the fire or overheat condition is gone, the resistance of the core material in the Kidde system will increase to the reset point and the flight deck indications go away.

_____ 9. Pneumatic continuous loop systems are used for engine fire detection of reciprocating type aircraft and have the same function as the Kidde system; however they work on a different principle.

_____ 10. The Lindberg fire/overheat detector's sensor tube also contains a hydrogen filled core material.

MULTIPLE CHOICE

1. Name the classes of fires that are likely to occur onboard aircraft
    a. Class 1, 2, 3, and 4
    b. Class I, II, III, and IV
    c. Class A, B, C, and D
    d. Class red, blue, green, and yellow

2. Regarding the Statements below:
    #1 The Kidde system uses a slender Inconel tube packed with thermally
        sensitive eutectic salt and a nickel wire center conductor.
    #2 In the Lindberg continuous-loop system, two wires are imbedded
        in an inconel tube filled with a thermistor core material.

    a. Statement 1 and 2 are true
    b. Statement 1 and 2 are false
    c. Statement 1 is true and statement 2 is false
    d. Statement 1 is false and statement 2 is true

3. If the temperature of the Kidde continuous loop core _____ the electrical resistance to ground _____
    a. increases, decreases
    b. decreases, increases
    c. Increases, increases
    d. decreases, decreases

4. Single point pneumatic detectors that are used in some turboprop aircraft are based on the principles of
    _____ laws.
    a. Thermal
    b. Gas
    c. Newton's
    d. Hydraulic

5. Lindberg fire detection systems use a loop system that is filled with a _____ and use a _____ to actuate the control circuitry.
    a. Thermistor material, pressure diaphragm
    b. Thermistor material, thermocouple
    c. Gas, thermocouple
    d. Gas, pressure diaphragm

6. The Lindberg continuous fire detection uses _____ gas.
    a. Helium
    b. Argon
    c. Oxygen
    d. Nitrogen

7. What type of fire extinguishing agent is an ozone depleting and global warming chemical and its production has been banned by international agreement?
    a. Nitrogen
    b. Helium
    c. CO2
    d. Halon

8. What type of fire extinguishing agent is used to fight Class A, B, or C fires?
    a. CO2
    b. Halocarbon clean agents
    c. Dry powder
    d. Answer 2 and 3 are correct

9. The most common extinguishing agent still used today is?
    a. CO2
    b. Halon 1201
    c. Halon 1301
    d. dry powder

10. The cartridge service life recommended by the manufacturer is usually in terms of _____.
    a. days
    b. years
    c. months
    d. flight cycles

1. Name 5 typical zones on aircraft that have a fixed fire detection and/or fire extinguisher system?

2. What types of systems are used to detect fires in reciprocating engine and small turboprop aircraft?

3. What types of systems are used to detect fire in turbine engine fire protection systems?

4. Name 3 types of continuous loop fire detection systems.

5. What are the advantages of using Support tube mounted sensing elements?

6. What type of fire detection and extinguishing systems are controlled by advanced detection system circuitry?

7. What type of extinguishing agents are used for a class A, B, and C fire?

8. Transport aircraft have fixed fire extinguishing systems installed in:

9. What is installed in the outlet of the discharge valve?

10. What is the function of the cartridge (squib) that is installed in the discharge valve?

11. What is the purpose of the Yellow disk discharge indicator?

12. What will happen when the fire switch is activated?

13. What is a Class A cargo or baggage compartment?

14. What is the difference between a Class A and a Class B cargo and baggage compartment?

15. What indications will occur in the cockpit if there is smoke in a cargo compartment?

16. What could be the results of kinks and sharp bends in the sensing element?

17. Using the pressure chart below. What is the minimum pressure when the temperature is 70°F?

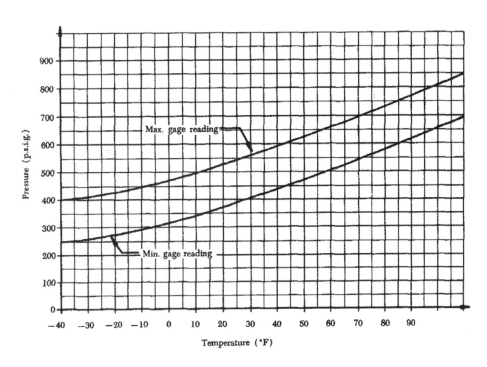

Fire extinguisher pressure graph

1. A squib, as used in a fire protection system is a:
   a. temperature sensing device
   b. device for causing the fire extinguishing agent to be released
   c. probe used for installing frangible disks in extinguisher bottles

2. When used in fire detection systems having a single indicator light, thermal switches are wired in:
   a. parallel with each other and in series with the light
   b. series with each other and the light
   c. series with each other and parallel with the light

3. Regarding the following statements in reference to aircraft fire extinguishing systems:
   (1) during removal or installation, the terminals of discharge cartridges should be grounded or shorted.
   (2) before connecting cartridge terminals to the electrical system, the system should be checked with a voltmeter to see that no voltage exists at the terminal connections.

   a. only number 2 is true
   b. both number 1 and number 2 are true
   c. neither number 1 nor number 2 are true

4. Referring to the chart below , determine the temperature range for a fire extinguishing agent storage container with a pressure of 330 PSIG. (Consider 330 PSIG for both minimum and maximum pressure.)
   a. 47 to 73 °F
   b. 47 to 71 °F
   c. 45 to 73 °F

CONTAINER PRESSURE VERSUS TEMPERATURE		
TEMPERATURE ° F	CONTAINER PRESSURE (PSI)	
	MINIMUM	MAXIMUM
-40	60	145
-30	83	165
-20	105	188
-10	125	210
0	145	230
10	167	252
20	188	275
30	209	295
40	230	317
50	255	342
60	284	370
70	319	405
80	356	443
90	395	483
100	438	523

5. What method is used to detect the thermal discharge of a built-in fire extinguisher system?
    a. A discoloring of the yellow plastic disk in the thermal discharge line
    b. A rupture of the red plastic disk in the thermal discharge line
    c. The thermal plug missing from the side of the bottle

6. The thermal switches of a bimetallic thermal switch type fire detection system are heat sensitive units that complete circuits at a certain temperature. They are connected in_____ .
    a. parallel with each other, and in parallel with the indicator lights
    b. parallel with each other, but in series with the indicator lights
    c. series with each other, but in parallel with the indicator lights

7. Referring to the chart above, determine what pressure is acceptable for a fire extinguisher when the surrounding area temperature is 33 °F. (Rounded to the nearest whole number.)
    a. 215 to 302 PSIG
    b. 214 to 301 PSIG
    c. 215 to 301 PSIG

8. On a periodic check of fire extinguisher containers, the pressure was not between minimum and maximum limits. What procedure should be followed?
    a. release pressure if above limits
    b. replace the extinguisher container
    c. increase pressure if below limits

9. In some fire extinguishing systems, evidence that the system has been intentionally discharged is indicated by the absence of a:
    a. red disk on the side of the fuselage
    b. green disk on the side of the fuselage
    c. yellow disk on the side of the fuselage

10. The thermocouple fire warning system is activated by a:
    a. certain temperature
    b. core resistance drop
    c. rate of temperature rise

11. Maintenance of fire detection systems includes the :
    a. repair of damaged sensing elements
    b. removal of excessive loop or element material
    c. replacement of damaged sensing elements

12. A carbon dioxide (CO_2) hand held fire extinguisher may be used on an electrical fire if the:
    a. horn is nonmetallic
    b. handle is insulated
    c. horn is nonmagnetic

13. Which fire extinguishing agent is considered to be the least toxic?
    a. carbon dioxide
    b. bromotrifluoromethane (Halon 1301)
    c. bromochloromethane (Halon 1011)

14. Which fire detection system measures temperature rise compared to a reference temperature?
    a. fenwal continuous loop
    b. Lindberg continuous element
    c. thermocouple

15. In what area of an aircraft would you find a carbon monoxide detector?
    a. surface combustion heater compartment
    b. cockpit and/or cabin
    c. engine and/or nacelle

16. What occurs when a visual smoke detector is activated?
    a. A warning bell within the indicator alarms automatically
    b. A lamp within the indicator illuminates automatically
    c. The test lamp illuminates and an alarm is provided automatically

17. The types of fire extinguishing agents for aircraft interior fires are
    a. water, carbon dioxide, dry chemical, and halogenated hydrocarbons
    b. water, dry chemical, methyl bromide, and chlorobromomethane
    c. water, carbon tetrachloride, carbon dioxide, and dry chemical

18. When air samples contain carbon monoxide, portable carbon monoxide detectors containing yellow silica gel will turn which color?
    a. blue
    b. green
    c. red

19. Smoke detection instruments are classified by their method of:
    a. construction
    b. maintenance
    c. detection

20. Smoke in the cargo and/or baggage compartment of an aircraft is commonly detected by which instrument?
    a. chemical reactor
    b. photoelectric cell
    c. sniffer

21. A contaminated carbon monoxide portable test unit would be returned to service by :
    a. heating the indicating element to 300° F to reactivate the chemical
    b. installing a new indicating element
    c. evacuating the indicating element with CO2

22. A thermocouple in a fire detection system causes the warning system to operate because:
    a. it generates a small current when heated
    b. heat decreases its electrical resistance
    c. it expands when heated and forms a ground for the warning system

23. The proper fire extinguishing agent to use on an aircraft brake fire is:
    a. water
    b. carbon dioxide
    c. dry powder chemical

24. Why does the Fenwal fire detection system use spot detectors wired parallel between two separate circuits?
    a. a control unit is used to isolate the bad system in case of malfunction
    b. this installation is equal to two systems: a main system and a reserve system
    c. a short may exist in either circuit without causing a false fire warning

25. A fire extinguisher container can be checked to determine its charge by :
    a. attaching a remote pressure gauge
    b. weighing the container and its contents
    c. a hydrostatic test

Answers

Answers to Study Aid questions and Knowledge Application questions (sections 1 & 2 of each chapter) are given in the following pages. Answers to the Final Chapter are given only on the corresponding Instructor support CD.

CHAPTER 1

FILL IN THE BLANKS

1. structural member
2. torsion, shear
3. pounds per square inch, psi
4. full cantilever
5. spanwise
6. longerons
7. web, cap
8. firewall, engine
9. regulate engine temperature
10. lateral, longitudinal, and directional
11. flutter
12. left
13. lateral or horizontal
14. Right
15. fowler
16. AOA or angle of attack
17. spoilers
18. zero station
19. stainless steel
20. up and down, back and forth

TRUE/FALSE

1. false - wing spar
2. false - tension
3. true
4. false - stringers
5. false - skin carries load
6. true
7. false - ribs forward of front spar used for shaping and strengthening leading edge
8. true
9. true
10. false - electrical and hydraulic power
11. false - wing sealed with fuel resistant sealing
12. true
13. false - installed and operate dependently
14. false - winglets
15. false - conventional and tailwheel
16. true
17. true
18. false - tilting the rotor
19. false - flap
20. false - opposite direction of rotation

MATCHING

1. A - Exhaust valve
2. F - Intake valve

KNOWLEDGE APPLICATION

1. Rotors are rotating wings as opposed to propellers and rotating airfoils of an engine
2. The degree of deformation of a material

3. The part is shortened or compressed on the inside of the bend and stretched on the outside of the bend. This is a combination of compression and tension stress.
4. They must be streamlined to meet aerodynamic requirements to reduce drag or direct airflow
5. Members such as beams, struts, bars, and longerons covered with fabric.
6. Maintaining the proper amount of strength while keeping the weight within the allowable limits
7. Monocoque fuselages have heavy structural members located at intervals with no other bracing members, requiring the skin to carry the primary loads. Semi-monocoque type fuselage uses longerons as longitudinal reinforcements that help support the skin.
8. Metal fatigue is caused by cycling from pressurized to unpressurized and back during each flight as well as withstanding the pressure differential in-flight
9. Jury struts subdue strut movement and oscillation on struts that are attached to the wings at a great distance from the fuselage. They are vertical support structures that are attached to the wing and strut.
10. They are the principal structural member and they support all distributed loads as well as concentrated weights (i.e. fuselage, landing gear, engines, etc.)
11. They are located entirely forward of the front spar and they are used to shape and strengthen the wing leading edge. They do not span the entire wing chord.
12. They are streamlined and house the engine and its components. They can sometimes be designed to house the landing gear. All nacelles incorporate a firewall to isolate the engine from the rest of the airframe. They have cowlings which cover areas that can be easily accessed when detached.
13. Lateral- elevators, longitudinal- ailerons, vertical-rudder
14. Camber and lift are increased
15. Slots direct air over the upper surface of the wing during high angles of attack. They lower stall speed and provide control during slow flight. Slots are located on the outer leading edge of the wing forward of the ailerons.
16. Typically linked directly to the control surface so they move automatically when the control surface moves. Balance tabs aide the pilot in overcoming the force needed to move the control surface
17. Allows for greater clearance between the propeller, which were longer back then, and loose debris when operating on unpaved runway
18. The two main wheels are forward of the center of gravity while the tail is aft. If the aircraft swerves on landing the tail can swing out pulling the center of gravity aft of the main wheels allowing the tail to freely pivot
19. As the plane of rotation of the rotor blade tilts the advancing blade has a greater relative windspeed compared to the retreating blade. This causes a greater amount of lift being developed on the advancing blade resulting in the blade flapping up. The opposite occurs on the retreating side causing the blade to flap down.

20. Stands for "no tail rotor" because it has an engine driven adjustable fan located in the tail boom. As the speed of the main rotor changes, the speed of the NOTAR fan changes as well. Air is vented out of two long slots on the right side of the tail to counteract the torque produced by the main rotor.

CHAPTER 2

FILL IN THE BLANKS

1. Force, dyne
2. Hg or inches of mercury, barometer
3. Increases, increases, increases
4. Inversely, directly
5. First, inertia
6. Increase
7. upper surface
8. AOA or angle of attack
9. Longitudinal
10. Fluid, pressure
11. High, low, outward, vortex
12. Static
13. Ailerons, elevator, rudder
14. Free-spinning, upward
15. Down
16. Left, all
17. Dissymmetry
18. Clutch
19. Right, left
20. "Go" and "no-go"
21. Fairleads, 3°
22. Turnbuckle, left-hand
23. Position or angle, wing tips
24. Dihedral, incidence
25. Double-twist, single-wire

TRUE or FALSE

1. true
2. true
3. false; faster at higher altitude
4. false; inversely
5. true
6. true
7. false; lift to drag ratio
8. false; drag, not weight
9. true
10. false; center of gravity
11. false; vertical axis
12. true
13. false; wing fences
14. true
15. true
16. false weight added fore or aft of hinges
17. false; manufacturer provides instructions for fabrication
18. true
19. false; issued by FAA
20. false; flexible and used for pulleys
21. false; not used
22. true
23. true
24. true
25. false; never re-used

KNOWLEDGE APPLICATION

1. It is a substance that has the ability to flow or assume the shape of the container in which it is enclosed.

2. Atmospheric pressure is the force exerted against the earth's surface by the weight of the air above that surface. It is measured using a barometer in "Hg.

3. Density varies in direct proportion with pressure and inversely with temperature.

4. Absolute - the weight of water vapor in a unit volume of air; Relative - the ratio (%) of the moisture actually in the air to the moisture it would hold if it were saturated at the same temperature and pressure.

5. The law of action and reaction states that for every action (force) there is an equal and opposite reaction (force).

6. The top part of the wing has a greater curvature than the bottom. This requires the air above the wing to travel farther than the bottom. The air therefore, has a greater velocity and a decreased pressure. The pressure differential creates lift. The high pressure on the bottom of the wing tries to equalize by rising to the low pressure area.

7. There is an area of negative pressure behind the resultant force when AOA is 0°. As AOA increases towards its critical point, the resultant force moves forward. Once critical angle is reached the resultant force falls rapidly until the wing stalls.

8. Drag is the resistance of the air to an object moving through it. There are 3 forms of drag: Parasite drag occurs when an exposed object offers resistance to the air. Profile drag is the parasite drag of the airfoil. Induced drag occurs as lift is created and the air flow spillage over the wing tip creates a vortex. This vortex constitutes induced drag.

9. Control is the pilot action of moving the flight controls, providing the aerodynamic force that induces the aircraft to follow a desired flight path. Controllability means that the aircraft responds easily and promptly to movement of the flight controls.

10. Sharp disturbances generate shock waves that affect lift and drag as well as airflow downstream of the shockwave. A cone of pressure which moves outward and rearward from the shockwave. Also, the energy of the object moving excites the chemical bonds of the oxygen and nitrogen.

11. Each blade can move back and forth in plane, lead and lag; and flap up and down through a hinge independent of the other blades.

12. As the engine turns the main rotor in a counterclockwise direction, the helicopter fuselage tends to turn the opposite direction. The action of the main rotor blade creates an equal and opposite force that turns the fuselage clockwise.

13. It is a mechanical connection between the collective lever and engine throttle. When the collective lever is raised, power increases and when lowered, power is decreased. This system maintains RPM close to the desired value.

14. Loose elevator linkage at swash plate horn, loose elevator, or tail rotor balance and track

15. The gas producer (compressor turbine) is essentially disconnected from the power turbine. When the engine is started, there is little resistance from the power turbine allowing the gas turbine to accelerate to normal idle without the transmission load dragging it down.

16. Pulleys are used to guide cables and change cable direction. Pulley guards prevent jamming or the cable slipping off when slackened due to temperature changes.

17. Positioning the flight controls in the neutral position and locking them in place. Adjusting the cable tension and maintaining control surface neutral. Adjusting the control stops to the aircraft manufacturer's specifications.

18. To make minor adjustments in cable length and for adjusting cable tension.

19. Trim tab systems. As the trim tab control moves, the cable drum winds or unwinds to actuate the trim tab cables.

20. Annual, 100-hour inspection, progressive

CHAPTER 3

FILL IN THE BLANKS

1. Cotton, sag, doping or nitrate doping
2. 5-10
3. Polyester
4. Pinking shears, unraveling
5. Unairworthy
6. One-time
7. UV light
8. Retarder
9. Fasteners, airflow
10. Organic
11. Weight, stresses
12. Rejuvenator, airworthy
13. Exposed, 1.25 or 1 ¼"
14. Blanket, precut or pre-sewn
15. Temperature, humidity
16. Volume, pressure
17. Durability, appearance
18. Propeller wash, one rib
19. Inspection or maintenance, inspection
20. Patches, strut

TRUE or FALSE

1. false; along the length of fabric
2. true
3. false; FAA issued
4. true
5. false; different thread
6. true
7. true
8. true
9. false; all coatings should be removed
10. false; not an FAA approved method
11. true
12. true
13. true
14. true
15. false; dope or glue
16. true
17. false skipping from one end to the other and the middle
18. true
19. false; the widest - 4"
20. true

KNOWLEDGE APPLICATION

1. They created a system of combining nitrate dope and butyrate dope. The fabric was first coated with nitrate dope for adhesion and protective qualities and then butyrate dope was added reducing the overall flammability.
2. Appendix A states that changing parts of an aircraft wing, tail surface, or fuselage when not listed in the aircraft specifications issued by the FAA is a major alteration and requires a Form 337
3. It is a self-adhesive cloth tape that is used on sharp protrusions, rib caps, metal seams, and other areas to provide a smoother surface to keep fabric from being torn.
4. Hand thread is 3-ply, uncoated polyester thread with a 15-lb tensile strength; machine thread is 4-ply with a 10-lb tensile strength
5. With a hot soldering pencil that also heat seals the fabric through the center of the fabric.
6. The blanket method uses multiple flat sections of fabric trimmed and attached to the airframe. Each aircraft is considered differently to determine size and layout of the blankets but it is typical for a small blanket to be cut for each

small surface. Fabric is adhered to the airframe using approved adhesive, and specific manufacturer's instructions.
7. Eye protection, respirator, skin protection, and ventilation
8. A sheet of felt or polyester padding may be used before the fabric is applied. Approved padding ensures compatibility with the adhesives and first coating of the covering process.
9. Fabrics is shrunk in stages, using lower temperature first. The first shrink removes wrinkles and excess fabric. The final shrinkage gives the desired tautness. Fabric should be shrunk by skipping from one end to the other and then the middle to achieve uniform tautness.
10. Drain grommets allows for an escape of rain water and condensation from under the fabric. They are located at the lowest part of each structural area and each rib bay of the wings. Specific locations of each drain grommet can be found in the AC 43.13 or STC.
11. Chordwise tape is applied first followed by spanwise tape.
12. It is a coat used in some approved covering processes that combines the sealer and fill coats into one. They surround and seal the fabric fibers, provide a good adhesion for following coats, and have UV blocking agents.

CHAPTER 4

FILL IN THE BLANKS

1. strong, cracks
2. shear, torsion
3. parallel, three
4. bearing, shear
5. parallel, double-cut
6. shape, half-round
7. pneumatic, electric
8. stops, underlying
9. bends
10. press, complex
11. feed, curvature
12. deburr, stretching
13. V-blocks, flanges
14. thickness, temper
15. K-factor, 90°
16. relief holes, tangent
17. excellent, feed
18. load
19. manufacturing, conventional
20. bulbed, locking (foil)
21. regulated, torque
22. aluminum, clearance
23. sleeves, protruding
24. less, thickest
25. pitch, adjacent
26. knife-edge, enlarging
27. perpendicular, weight
28. spar, strength
29. rivet gage
30. hot, flow

KNOWLEDGE APPLICATION

1-1. d	1-2. c	1-3. f
1-4. e	1-5. a	1-6. b
1-7. a	1-8. f	1-9. e
1-10. c	1-11. b	
2-1. l	2-2. c	2-3. i
2-4. q	2-5. f	2-6. a
2-7. e	2-8. o	2-9. g

2-10. d	2-11. p	2-12. j
2-13. m	2-14. r	2-15. b
2-16. h	2-17. n	2-18. k
3-1. d	3-2. f	3-3. b
3-4. g	3-5. a	3-6. i
3-7. e	3-8. h	3-9. c
4-1. c	4-2. a	4-3. e
4-4. d	4-5. g	4-6. b
4-5. f		
5-1. e	5-2. a	5-3. c
5-4. f	5-5. b	5-6. d
6-1. h	6-2. l	6-3. d
6-4. p	6-5. i	6-6. n
6-7. f	6-8. a	6-9. k
6-10. b	6-11. o	6-12. e
6-13. j	6-14. g	6-15. m
6-16. c		
7-1. f	7-2. b	7-3. e
7-4. a	7-5. d	7-6. c
8-1. b	8-2. e	8-3. a
8-4. d	8-5. g	8-6. c
8-7. f	8-8. f	8-9. c
8-10. g	8-11. e	8-12. b
8-13. a		

9-1. 2D	9-2. 2D + 1/16"
9.3. 2.5D	9-4. 2.5D + 1/16"

10-1. 3D	10-2. 3D + 1/16"
10-3. 4D	10-4. 4D + 1/16"
10-5. 3.5D	10-6. 3.5D + 1/16"
10-7. 4.5D	10-8. 4.5D + 1/16"

CHAPTER 5

FILL IN THE BLANKS

1. gas, electric arc, electric resistance
2. 6300, acetylene, oxygen
3. stir welding
4. metal inert gas (MIG) welding
5. DC straight polarity, AC
6. spot, seam
7. argon, argon/helium or argon/nitrogen
8. colorless, odorless, tasteless
9. green, right hand
10. temperature
11. upright, liquid acetone
12. bigger
13. neutral, carburizing, and oxidizing
14. 6300, oxygen
15. backfire, overheating, loose
16. acetylene, oxygen
17. low carbon, low alloy
18. flux
19. silver, oxygen
20. foot pedal, torch mounted
21. longitudinally, radially
22. AC, cleaning action, surface oxides
23. color, silver
24. bead, groove, fillet, and lap joint

25. warping, a buckling
26. inner
27. formed steel patch plate
28. split sleeve
29. nonrepairable, welded
30. larger diameter

TRUE or FALSE

1. false. gas, electric arc, and electric resistance welding.
2. false. Most common for material under 3/16
3. true
4. true
5. false. The rod is not consumed during welding
6. true. Plasma arc can cut all electrically conductive metals.
7. false. Never higher than 15 psi.
8. true
9. false. prevents a high pressure flame or fuel mixture being pushed back into either cylinder causing an explosion.
10. true
11. false. The light intensity of arc welding is much higher and different lenses are required.
12. false; welding tips have one hole; cutting tips several holes
13. false. open acetylene valve before the oxygen valve.
14. true; neutral flame at 5,850 °F; carburizing flame at 5,700
15. false; Always turn off the acetylene valve first
16. true
17. false. Maintain a neutral flame for most steels and a slight excess of acetylene for stainless steel
18. true
19. false; magnesium is done with a neutral flame.
20. false; Thoriated and zirconiated electrodes have better electron emission characteristics.
21. true
22. false; DC straight polarity
23. true
24. true
25. false; use welded split sleeve reinforcements.

KNOWLEDGE APPLICATION

1. Gas shielded arc welding.
2. If ignited it is extremely hard to extinguish.
3. The weld zone must be shielded with an inert gas.
4. To have the base metal chemically clean without the slightest film of oxide.
5. A neutral flame.
6. Weld a formed steel patch plate over the dented area.
7. Cool the inner sleeve with dry ice or in cold water.
8. By using a larger tip and adjusting the pressures.
9. Gas shielded arc welding.
10. The acetylene, to allow gas in the tip to burn out.
11. Tack welding at intervals along the joint.
12. Turn off the valves and relieve all pressure.
13. They must be re-heat treated.
14. A low strength weld.
15. metallic arc welding.
16. A gas is used as a shield around the arc to prevent the atmosphere from contaminating the weld.
17. The weld is stronger, more ductile, and more corrosion resistant.

CHAPTER 6

FILL IN THE BLANKS

1. 8-12%, 20%
2. decay, musty, moldy
3. temperature, humidity, deterioration
4. shear
5. decay, rot, decay
6. water penetration
7. compression
8. sharp or solid
9. spruce
10. plywood
11. softwoods
12. grain direction
13. mineral streaks
14. cracks
15. compression
16. casein glue, plastic resin glue, resorcinol glue, epoxy
17. wetting tests
18. full strength, stress
19. scarf joints
20. wing attachment, landing gear, engine mount fittings.

TRUE or FALSE

1. true: a certificated mechanic may not perform work unless he has performed the work concerned at an earlier date.
2. false: ideal range is 8-12%.
3. true
4. false: Shear loads
5. true
6. false: The condition of the fabric provides an useful indication of the condition of the wood underneath.
7. true
8. true: A soft and mushy area is an indication of rotting.
9. false: Spruce is the preferred choice.
10. false: softwoods
11. true
12. false: Hard knots are acceptable under certain conditions.
13. false
14. true
15. true
16. false: Surfaces should be prepared with a planer or joiner.
17. true
18. false: any point except at wing attachment fittings, landing gear , engine mount, or lift and interplace strut fittings.
19. true
20. true

KNOWLEDGE APPLICATION

1. Two or more layers glued together with the grain of all layers approximately parallel.
2. It is usually made of an odd number of thin plies with the grain of each layer at 45 or 90 degrees to the adjacent ply or plies. Laminated wood all grain are parallel.
3. Spruce
4. Inspect for a dark discoloration of the wood surface or gray stains along the grain.
5. Casein (obsolete), plastic resin glue, resorcinol glue, and epoxy resin.
6. Curing time as well as joint strength. Curing time will be shorter and the joint strength will increase.
7. If inspection fails to reveal any decay.
8. Yes, hard knots up to ¾ inch in diameter are acceptable under certain conditions.
9. It is detrimental to strength and is difficult to recognize, compression wood is characterized by high specific gravity.

10. To determine whether or not they are harmless, or preliminary, or advanced decay.
11. prevent crushing the wood when the bolts are tightened.
12. weak and strong areas in the same joint.
13. Clamps, elastic straps, weight, vacuum bags, brads, nails, screws, and electric and hydraulic presses.
14. A scarf joint.
15. The effective glue area will be reduced if both beveled cuts are not the same.
16. The same type of plywood as the original.
17. The use of waxed paper or release films between the patch and pressure plate.
18. Under a wing attachment fitting, landing gear fitting, engine mount fitting, and lift and interplane strut fittings.
19. To provide additional bearing surface.
20. 70 F.

CHAPTER 7

FILL IN THE BLANKS

1. high strength; relatively low weight; corrosion resistance
2. fairings, control surfaces, landing gear doors, leading and trailing edge panels, interior components, floor beams and boards, stabilizer primary structure on new generation large aircraft, turbine engine fan blades, propellers.
3. fiber and matrix
4. wing spoilers; fairings; ailerons; flaps; nacelles; floor boards; rudders
5. insulating properties; energy absorption and/or redirection; smooth cell walls; moisture and chemical resistance; environmentally compatible; aesthetically pleasing; relatively low cost.
6. high compressive strength; resistance to water penetration.
7. delamination; resin starved areas; resin rich areas; blisters/air bubbles; wrinkles; voids; thermal decomposition
8. improper cure or processing; improper machining; mishandling; improper drilling; tool drops; contamination; improper sanding; substandard material; inadequate tooling; mislocation of holes or details.
9. interlaminar shear ; compression strength
10. scorches, stains, dents, penetration, abrasion, or chips
11. resin starvation, resin richness, wrinkles, ply bridging, discoloration (due to overheating, lightning strike, etc.), impact damage, foreign matter, blisters, disbonding
12. calibration; damage
13. dust; oil; vapors; smoke; moisture
14. secondary bonding
15. nylon; polyester
16. ability to slow or stop fatigue crack growth; replace lost structural area due to corrosion grind-outs; structurally enhance areas with small and negative margins.
17. vertical; controlled; no bleed out; horizontal (or edge)
18. strength requirements
19. potted
20. freeze
21. more
22. lightly loaded; small
23. fiberglass
24. wet lay up, prepreg, DVD, wet lay up
25. special storage, handling, curing
26. honeycomb sandwich, bearing
27. Hi loks, lockbolts
28. diamond coated, solid carbide, high speed steel
29. flush type
30. higher, lower

TRUE or FALSE

1. true
2. true
3. false; fiberglass yarns are twisted, Kevlar is not
4. false; Unidirectional Tape Fibers are held in place by the resin and have a higher strength than woven fabrics.
5. true
6. true
7. true
8. false; Carbon Fibers have a high potential for causing galvanic corrosion with metallic fasteners and structures.
9. true
10. true
11. true
12. true
13. true
14. true
15. true
16. false
17. false; when using the through transmission ultrasonic inspection method, areas with a greater loss than the reference standard indicate a defective area.
18. false; the handling life is shorter
19. true
20. true
21. false; in a resin starved repair
22. true
23. true
24. false
25. true
26. false
27. true
28. false
29. true
30. false

KNOWLEDGE APPLICATION

1. A homogeneous material has a uniform composition throughout and has no internal physical boundaries.
2. An anisotropic material has mechanical and/or physical properties that vary with direction relative to natural reference axes inherent in the material.
3. Quasi-isotropic material has approximately the same properties as isotropic. An example is a composite laminate with the fibers orientated in the 0°, 90°, +45°, and -45° direction to simulate isotropic properties
4. More flexibility for lay-up of complex shapes
5. Save weight; Minimize resin void size; Maintain fiber orientation during the fabrication process
6. nickel-coated graphite cloth; metal meshes; aluminum fiberglass; conductive paints
7. low smoke and flammability characteristics.
8. Three – A, B & C stage
9. In the frozen state the resin of the prepreg material will stay in the B stage of curing. The curing will start when the material is removed from the freezer and heated up again.
10. Panels with complex curves
11. Small core cells provide better support for sandwich face sheets. Higher density core is stronger and stiffer than lower density core.
12. too much resin is used. For non-structural applications this is not necessarily bad but it will add weight.
13. too much resin is bled off during the curing process or if not enough resin is applied during the wet lay-up process.

14. The method is accomplished by tapping the inspection area with a solid round disk or lightweight hammer-like device and listening to the response of the structure to the hammer.
15. A clear, sharp, ringing sound
16. A dull or thud-like sound
17. Changes within the internal elements of the structure might produce pitch changes that might be interpreted as defects, when in fact they are present by design.
18. Through transmission ultrasonic inspection uses two transducers, one on each side of the area to be inspected. The ultrasonic signal is transmitted from one transducer to the other transducer. The instrument then measures the loss of signal strength. The instrument shows the loss as a percent of the original signal strength or the loss in decibels. The signal loss is compared to a reference standard. Areas with a greater loss than the reference standard indicate a defective area.
19. Cover the unprotected sides of the prepreg material with parting film and clean the area being repaired immediately before laying up the repair plies.
20. two parts are simultaneously cured. A typical application is the simultaneous cure of a stiffener and a skin.
21. A permanent repair restores the required strength and durability, an interim repair only restores the required strength and has a different inspection interval.
22. A potting repair is heavier than the original control and this could affect the control balance and introduce flutter.
23. Water will boil at cure temperatures and could blow the facesheets of the core.
24. Two holes are drilled on the outside of the delamination area and a low-viscosity resin is injected in one hole till it flows out the other hole.
25. thick structures or structures made of carbon fiber or Kevlar would block the radar signals.
26. Place impregnated fabric in the debulking chamber and apply a vacuum bag over the lay up. Apply a vacuum to the chamber (box). Because of a vacuum their will not be any pressure applied to the lay up but volatiles will be removed. This will reduce voids in the lay up. Heat will be applied to lower the viscosity of the resin to help volatile removal. After debulking the vacuum in the outer chamber is removed and the lay up will be compacted by the atmospheric pressure. The patch will be staged at temperature. After the staging the patch will be removed and bonded to the aircraft with a past adhesive and cured with a heater blanket.

CHAPTER 8

FILL IN THE BLANKS

1. weight, integrity
2. Polyurethane
3. Dipping, brushing, and spraying
4. spray gun with integral paint container, spray gun with pressure pot
5. siphon feed gun, gravity feed gun, HVLP gun
6. internal, air, fluid
7. preparation
8. upper
9. Crosscoat
10. 50%
11. thinner, reducer
12. loose nozzle, clogged, packing
13. milky haze
14. trapped solvents, air, moisture
15. too much, too close, too slowly
16. bumpy

17. small holes
18. trapped solvents, unequal drying
19. too far, air pressure
20. 3 times

TRUE or FALSE

1. true
2. true
3. false; bright yellow
4. false; if the paint materials are too thin
5. true; 65% or more paint is transferred with HVLP spray gun.
6. false. A HVLP spray gun is an internal mix gun.
7. true
8. true
9. false. alodine is used to etch the aluminum material
10. true
11. false; if the spray pattern is offset to one side, the air port in the air cap or the ports in the horn may be plugged
12. true
13. false; first spray the corners and gaps
14. true
15. true
16. false; ensure the surface is clean
17. false; "N"
18. false; 12" high
19. false; it is old nitrocellulose finish
20. true

KNOWLEDGE APPLICATION

1. Primers, enamels, urethanes (polyurethane), and epoxies.
2. Environmental concerns; more effective primer formulas.
3. The spray pattern is offset to one side.
4. Bond to the surface, inhibit corrosion, and provide an anchor point for the finish coat
5. The use of respiratory protection such as fresh air supply or respirator. The use of protective clothing and gloves.
6. Dipping, brushing, and spraying.
7. Incorrect air pressure or the distance of the gun from the work is too large.
8. Too much paint being applied or gun too close to surface.
9. Incorrect paint viscosity, air pressure, gun setting, or distance of the gun from the work.
10. Clouding or blooming of the film.
11. Moisture in the air supply, adverse humidity, or changes in temperature.
12. Orange peel or pin holes due to too fast drying of paint.
13. Synthetic rubber products, composites, fabric, acrylics, and bonded surfaces.
14. It helps to eliminate general corrosion problems.
15. Polyurethane finishing system
16. Use a paint stripper, Plastic blast medium, or mechanical sanding (composite aircraft)
17. Open air valve all the way, set fluid valve to dial 4. Practice on a piece of masking paper and check if the fan shape and amount of paint applied are correct. Close the air valve if a smaller fan shape is required and open the fluid valve if more paint is required. Adjust both valves till the correct settings are achieved before starting the painting process.
18. A loose nozzle, clogged vent hole on the supply cup, or the packing may be leaking around the needle.
19. To ensure that the surface is clean and free from any type of contamination.
20. On the vertical tail surface or on the side of the fuselage.

CHAPTER 9

FILL IN THE BLANKS

1. mathematical, electricity
2. semiconductors, transistors
3. generators, alternators
4. conductor movement/force, magnetic field current
5. inverter, HZ (cycle) AC
6. Inductive, capacitance, phase
7. Inversely, reduced, half
8. impedance, resistance
9. lead-acid, ni-cad, plates
10. essential, thirty
11. potassium hydroxide, discharge, manufacturer's instructions
12. increases, greater, greater
13. generator control units (GCU), output
14. armature, field, electromagnetic, bus, loads
15. voltage/current, field
16. solid state, AC power, bus
17. alternator housing, integrated drive generator
18. bus power control unit, generator control unit
19. throttle, activated
20. flexing, stranded
21. mega-ohmmeter, condition
22. derating, %
23. voltage drop, satisfactory
24. one, staggered
25. switches, close

MATCHING

1. 1-c, 2-d, 3-b, 4-d, 5-a, 6-b
2. 1-a, 2-b, 3-b, 4-c, 5-a, 6-c
3. 1-c, 2-d, 3-c, 4-b, 5-a, 6-d, 7-c, 8-a, 9-b, 10-d
4. 1-c, 2-a, 3-b, 4-d, 5-b, 6-a, 7-c
5. 1-e, 2-c, 3-a, 4-f, 5-d, 6-b
6. 1-f, 2-c, 3-a, 4-d, 5-b, 6-e

KNOWLEDGE APPLICATION

1. 2.4A
2. 4 ohms
3. 24V
4. 24 x .707 = 17V
5. 112 x 1.41 = 158V
6. $X_L = 2\pi (60) (.175)$ $X_L = 66\Omega$
7. $R_T = \dfrac{1}{\frac{1}{10} + \frac{1}{15}}$ $R_T = 6\Omega$
8. $Z = \sqrt{R^2 + XL^2}$ $Z = \sqrt{8^2 + 8^2}$ $Z = 11.3\Omega$ (Use $X_L = 2\pi f L$ to find X_L in ohms) (use R=E/I to find R in ohms)
9. $Z = \sqrt{R^2 + XC^2}$ $Z = \sqrt{8^2 + 26.5^2}$ $Z = 28\Omega$
   (use $X_c = 1/(2\pi f c)$ to find X_c in ohms)
10. T.P. = $I^2 \times R$
11. Watts
12. $X_L = 2\pi (400)(.01)$ $X_L = 25\Omega$, $X_C = \dfrac{1}{2\pi \times 400 \times .00015}$
    $X_C = 2.65\Omega$, $Z = \dfrac{1}{\sqrt{\left(\frac{1}{40}\right)^2 + \left(\frac{1}{25} - \frac{1}{2.65}\right)^2}}$ $Z = 3\Omega$
13. A.P. = E x 1
14. Volt amps (VA)
15. T.P.= $5^2 \times 5.6$ T.P.= 140 Watts, A.P.= 50 x 5 A.P.= 250VA, PF= (140/250) X 100 PF=56%
16. in between 14 and 12, choose bigger size of 12.
17. size 20 wire
18. size 18 wire (in between 20 and 18)
19. 26.5A
20. 17.2A

CHAPTER 10

FILL IN THE BLANKS

1. senses; display
2. air; gyroscopes
3. bourbon tube, diaphragm or bellows, solid-state
4. sensed air pressure, digital values
5. pitot static, aircraft systems
6. altitude, pressure, pressure
7. true airspeed
8. machmeter
9. synchro
10. electro, permanent
11. crankshaft
12. tachometer probes, tach generator
13. forces, inertial reference
14. ADC
15. direction, angle
16. vacuum systems, pressure systems, electrical systems
17. artificial horizon, pitch, roll.
18. laterally, vertically, longitudinally
19. sensing elements, computing elements, output elements, command elements
20. attitude, electric attitude indicators
21. ECAM
22. flight management system (FMS)
23. flight, engine, airframe
24. 24
25. electromagnetic, electrical

TRUE or FALSE

1. true
2. false; flight, engine, navigation
3. true
4. false; an aneroid
5. false; remote
6. true
7. true
8. true
9. false; direct current systems often use DC Selsyn systems.
10. true
11. true
12. false; pushes the control yoke forwards to lower the nose
13. true
14. false; total air temperature is the static air temperature plus any rise in temperature caused by high speed movement of the aircraft through the air.
15. true
16. false; swinging the compass is the process for adjusting magnetic deviation.
17. true
18. false; the magnetic compass is not a sensing element of the autopilot system.
19. true
20. false; attitude indicator and directional gyro.
21. true
22. true
23. false; the master caution light can be cancelled.
24. false; low frequency
25. true

KNOWLEDGE APPLICATION

1. aircraft specification; type certificate data sheets; flight manuals
2. caution
3. a sensitive altimeter
4. scale, hysteresis, and installation
5. rate of climb, airspeed, and altimeter
6. a leak test
7. vacuum, air pressure, or electricity
8. transmits information from one point to another point
9. crankshaft or main turbine rotor speed
10. a thermocouple-type system
11. correct for deviations by adjusting compensating magnets
12. flight instruments, engine instruments, navigation instruments
13. the total exhaust pressure to the pressure of the ram air at the inlet of the engine
14. air data computer (ADC)
15. vane type which uses an alpha vane externally mounted to the outside of the fuselage; probe type which uses two slots in a probe that extends out of the side of the fuselage
16. cylinder head temperature in reciprocating engines and exhaust gas temperature in turbine engines
17. EICAS
18. EICAS
19. certificated A & P mechanics can remove, inspect, troubleshoot, and perform operation checks of instruments
20. EICAS or ECAM, Air DATA Computer, thrust management computer, EIFIS symbol generators, ADFS, Inertial reference system, collision avoidance system, radio navigational aids.

CHAPTER 11

FILL IN THE BLANKS

1. valence shells
2. holes, eight
3. shockley, three-layer
4. power, inverter
5. polarity, channel
6. open, closed
7. LEDs, color
8. ratio, base
9. base, larger
10. NAND
11. upper, horizontal situation
12. 90°, 90°
13. carrier, frequency
14. superior, radio
15. detector/demodulator
16. polarized, direction
17. conductive, antenna(s)
18. frequency, Morse code
19. NDB, null
20. RMI
21. glideslope, 3°
22. radar beacon, location
23. avoidance, transponder
24. radome
25. three, latitude/longitude

TRUE or FALSE

1. False, certified repair station
2. False, continuous
3. true
4. true
5. true
6. false; conductor
7. true
8. false; directly proportional
9. true
10. false; base

11. false; less
12. true
13. false high current gains
14. false; magnetic
15. true
16. true
17. false
18. false; inversely proportional
19. true
20. false; 136.975 MHz
21. true
22. false; stable oscillating frequency
23. true
24. false; 90° to the length of the antenna
25. false, 2°
26. false; inactive
27. true
28. false; 7500
29. false; AGL
30. true

KNOWLEDGE APPLICATION

1. changing signal's amplitude, frequency, or phase
2. size and inability to withstand vibration made them susceptible to damage.
3. Combines readily with itself and form a lattice of atoms in which adjacent atoms share electrons to fill out the valence shell. Can be easily doped to create N-type and P-type semiconductor material.
4. The negative battery terminal is attached to the p- material and attracts holes away from the junction in the diode. Positive terminal attached to the N- material attracting the free electrons from in the opposite direction. Current cannot flow through the circuit when this occurs.
5. When reversed biased, only leakage current flows through the diode unless it is equipped with a zener voltage. When the zener voltage is reached the diode lets current flow freely through the diode in the direction it is normally blocked. Zener diodes can be used to as a means of dropping voltage or voltage regulation as well as step down circuit voltage for a particular application.
6. Stable in a wide range of temperatures; reduce the overall number of components used saving money and increasing reliability.
7. Switching devices and SCR (with a slight modification)
8. Common-emitter amplifier; common-collector amplifier; common-base amplifier
9. If the input to the gate is Logic 1 then the output is NOT logic 1. A NOT gate inverts the input signal. If there is voltage at the input, there would be no output voltage.
10. In an OR gate if any one of the Logic inputs is a 1 then the output will be a 1. In EXCLUSIVE if both logic inputs are 1 then the output is 0 instead of 1.
11. An AC generator is placed at the midpoint of an antenna. As current builds and collapses in the antenna, a magnetic field does so around it. An electric field also builds and subsides as the voltage shifts from one end of the antenna to the other. Both fields fluctuate around the antenna at the same time. At any point along the antenna, voltage and current vary inversely to each other. Each new current flow creates new fields around the antenna that forces the not-totally-collapsed fields from the aircraft out into space
12. Process of removing the original information signal from the carrier wave.
13. FM has a steady current flow and requires less power to produce, since modulating an oscillator takes less power than modulating the amplitude.

14. Original carrier wave, carrier wave plus the modulating frequency, carrier wave minus modulating frequency
15. A receiver is needed to isolate the desired carrier wave with its information. It separates data signal from the carrier wave. It amplifies the desired frequency captured by the antenna which is weak from traveling through atmosphere.
16. Length, polarization, and directivity
17. A metal fuselage creates a ground plane that acts as the missing one-quarter length.
18. The orientation of electric and electromagnetic fields remain at 90°, but radiate from the antenna with varying strength in different directions. The strength of the radiated field varies depending on the type of antenna and the angular proximity to it. All antennas radiate a stronger signal in some directions compared to others.
19. A dipole antenna is a conductor and sometimes known as the Hertz antenna. AC transmission current is fed to a dipole antenna. Current is strongest in the middle of the antenna about half the wavelength of the transmission frequency in length. It is horizontally polarized. Common as VOR antenna. Marconi antennas are 1/4 wave for VHF communication. They are vertically polarized and create omnidirectional field. Loop antennas are, as their name implies, fashioned into a loop which alters its field characteristics significantly. It is more compact and less prone to damage. It is used as a receiving antenna and is highly direction-sensitive.
20. Bearing degrees to or from the station
21. Localizer-provides horizontal guidance to the centerline of the runway; glideslope-provides vertical guidance to the touchdown point; compass locator aids in intercepting the approach navigation aid system; marker beacon-provides distance-from-the-runway.
22. It transmits in such a way that the aircraft's target symbol is highlighted on the PPI to be distinguishable.
23. Required internationally in aircraft with more than 30 seats or more than 15000 kg. It provides advisories similar to TCAS I but also analyzes the flightpath of approaching aircraft.
24. Entire airspace covered at lower expense. Provides more accurate data as vector state is generated from the aircraft. Weather is a reduced factor. Ultra-high frequency GPS is not affected. Increased accuracy allows higher density traffic flow. The higher degree of control enables routing for fewer weather delays and optimum fuel burn rates.
25. Space segment, control segment, and user segment

CHAPTER 12

FILL IN THE BLANKS

1. 100, negligible
2. mineral, polyalphaolefin, phosphate ester
3. Skydrol, IV, V
4. seals, gaskets, hoses
5. micron, particle
6. cold start, pump ripples, shock loads
7. engine gearbox, electric motor
8. non-pressurized, bleed air
9. screening straining, preventing
10. cleaning, replacing
11. differential, operating principle, loaded
12. manually reset, permanent
13. power-driven, hand, engine driven
14. positive, non-positive
15. shear, in the middle of, smaller
16. electrically, servo, servo
17. diverts, pressure

219

18. priority, non-critical, low
19. burst, preserves
20. failure, rupture, excessive
21. thermal, thermal expansion
22. regulators, pump
23. shuttle, seal off
24. system, components
25. preload

TRUE or FALSE
1. false, 3000-5000
2. true
3. false, all contaminants are bad
4. false, filters cleaned or replaced
5. false, all of the following
6. true
7. false, non-pressurized
8. false, 5 microns
9. true
10. false, compensator controlled
11. true
12. true
13. true
14. true
15. true

KNOWLEDGE APPLICATION
1. Red
2. Material will be damaged, softened and/or peeled
3. A shear section in the pump-drive shaft
4. All lines should be plugged or capped after disconnecting.
5. A clogged filter
6. Hand pumps, engine-driven pumps, electrically driven pumps, and air driven (bleed air).
7. Cabin pressurization, bleed air, aspirator and venture-tee, and hydraulic system pressure.
8. Limit amount of pressure preventing failure of components
9. To manage the output of the pump to maintain system pressure and allow the pump to turn without resistance.
10. An accumulator
11. To control the rate of airflow
12. To remove contamination and moisture
13. Make sure the air or preload has been discharged.
14. No. petroleum base and phosphate ester fluids will not mix. Neither are seals for one fluid useable with others.
15. In a closed center system the fluid is always pressurized when the pump runs and therefore it will be faster then the open center system that needs to be built up pressure. Since most aircraft applications require instantaneous operation, closed center systems are the most widely used.
16. The advantage of the powerpack is that there is no need for a centralized hydraulic power supply system and long stretches of hydraulic lines which reduces weight.
17. required because the reservoirs are often located in wheel wells or other non-pressurized areas of the aircraft and at high altitude there is not enough atmospheric pressure to move the fluid to the pump inlet.
18. By-pass relief valve opens if the filter clogs this will permit continued hydraulic flow and operation of aircraft systems.
19. Centrifugal and impeller pumps
20. The angle of the pump starts to decrease when the system pressure reaches about 2850 psi. The output of the pump will decrease to adjust to system demand.
21. System pressure will increase.

22. Some controlled by pressure, some mechanically, some by electric switches.
23. The PTU is able to transfer power but not fluid between two hydraulic systems. For instance if the engine driven pump in the #1 system is inoperative than system pressure in the number 2 can power the PTU to power the number 1 system.
24. EDV solenoid will move up creating a path for the outlet pressure (Ps) to reach the top of the compensator valve. The outlet pressure will push the compensator valve down and the output pressure will act on the yoke actuating piston and reduce the yoke angle and pump output is reduced to zero.
25. Pressure-reducing valves are used in hydraulic systems where it is necessary to lower the normal system operating pressure a specified amount.
26. a] Dampen pressure surges in the hydraulic system caused by actuation of a unit and the effort of the pump to maintain pressure at a preset level. b] Aid or supplement the power pump when several units are operating at once by supplying extra power from its "accumulated" or stored power. c] Store power for the limited operation of a hydraulic unit when the pump is not operating. d] Supply fluid under pressure to compensate for small internal or external (not desired) leaks which would cause the system to cycle continuously by action of the pressure switches continually "kicking in."
27. To provide electrical and hydraulic power if the aircraft loses electrical or hydraulic power.
28. When pressurized nitrogen is not directly used to actuate the landing gear actuators or brake units, it will apply the pressurized nitrogen to move hydraulic fluid to the actuator.
29. The engine driven pump won't be able to draw fluid from the tank, and only the AC driven pump can supply fluid to essential systems.

CHAPTER 13
FILL IN THE BLANKS
1. tail wheel , tandem , tricycle landing gear
2. fairings, wheel pants.
3. spring steel, aluminum, composite materials.
4. torque links, torque arms
5. locating cam assembly (centering cam)
6. camber
7. powerpack
8. emergency extension system
9. landing gear retraction test, swinging
10. shimmy damper
11. thermal plugs
12. torqued
13. lack of lubrication, bluish
14. excessive impact, indentations
15. top, right
16. transfer plate, rotors, stators
17. carbon disc brake
18. independent system, booster system, power brake system
19. hydraulic system
20. take off
21. skid, imminent
22. skidding
23. gravity, pressure
24. skidding
25. chevron

TRUE or FALSE
1. false; most use a nosewheel steering system
2. true

3. false; filled with nitrogen and hydraulic fluid.

4. false; nitrogen in the tires and the shock strut combine to smooth out bumps.

5. true

6. true

7. false; hydraulic pressure

8. true

9. false; on high performance; not small single engine aircraft

10. false; being down and locked

11. true

12. false; modern aircraft use two piece wheels

13. false; inner halves have provisions for brake rotors.

14. true; if the wheel bolts have failed the axle nut could be the only thing that keeps the wheel halves together.

15. true

16. false; segmented rotor disc brakes are used on large transport category aircraft

17. true

18. true

19. false; the anti skid system provides input to the autobrake system to prevent brake skid.

20. true

21. false; type VII tires are high performance for jet aircraft

22. true

23. false; 3 hours

24. false; deflate the tire before removing or probing any area where a foreign object is lodged.

25. true

KNOWLEDGE APPLICATION

1. Dry air or nitrogen, and hydraulic fluid.
2. Clean and inspect for damage and proper extension.
3. They keep the main landing gear wheels pointed in a straight ahead direction.
4. Hydraulic, or electrical.
5. A simple system consisting of mechanical linkage hooked to the rudder pedals.
6. A shimmy damper or in large aircraft using power steering the power steering actuators provide the dampening.
7. They reduce the pressure to the brakes and increase the volume of fluid flow.
8. Independent, power boost, and power control.
9. Pressurize the system.
10. A rubber O-ring between the two wheel halves.
11. Proper tire inflation
12. Rapid or uneven wear near the edge of tread, and creep or slip when the brakes are applied.
13. During an annual or other inspections, when landing gear components have been replaced, and after hard landings
14. Discoloration (blue color)
15. To bring a fast moving aircraft to a stop during ground roll without tire skidding.
16. To relieve air pressure when the tire overheats due to hard braking or extended taxing to prevent tire blowout.
17. Gravity and pressure methods.
18. Mechanical (cables, linkages), electrical, or hydraulic.
19. Nosewheel centering internal cams or external track.
20. Carbon brakes

CHAPTER 14

FILL IN THE BLANKS

1. hard engine starting, slow warm-up, slow
2. explode, detonate
3. vaporizes, carburetor
4. 30-40 °F, humid
5. explosion, pressure, temperature
6. lower, higher
7. main, auxiliary, surge
8. rigid removable tanks, bladder tanks, integral fuel
9. sump
10. wiring
11. gate, plug
12. quickly
13. engine driven fuel pump
14. positive, vapor lock
15. vane type
16. crossfeed system, fuel transfer
17. large, fuel system
18. micronic, 10-25
19. fuel heaters
20. Direct current (DC)
21. Stain, seep, heavy seep, running
22. 1/1/2 inches, 4 inches
23. dried and ventilated, combustible gas indicator
24. cloudy
25. Over the wing, pressure refueling

TRUE or FALSE

1. true
2. false; turbine fuel has a higher flash point than AVGAS
3. true
4. false; higher cylinder head temperature
5. true
6. false; Jet A is the most common
7. false; pump feed system
8. true
9. true
10. false; aircraft equipped with integral fuel tanks have fuel vent systems and fuel jettison systems dump fuel when the take off weight is higher than the landing weight
11. true
12. false; to the engine driven fuel pump
13. false; variable displacement pump
14. false; lowest part of the tank
15. true
16. true
17. false; electronic fuel quantity systems have no moving part which is one of their advantages
18. true
19. false; they measure fuel mass
20. true
21. false; must be repaired before the next flight because vapors in these areas could cause a fire or explosion
22. true
23. false; organisms do not grow in AVGAS, only turbine fuel
24. true
25. true

KNOWLEDGE APPLICATION

1. If take off weight is higher than the landing weight, in an emergency these aircraft need to reduce the weight to a specified landing weight.
2. Rigid removable cell, bladder-type cell, integral fuel cell
3. The structure of the cavity that the cell fits into.

4. alerts the flight crew that there may be danger of ice crystals forming in the fuel.

5. To provide an interconnected fuel system so that fuel can be fed from various tanks to any engine.

6. crossfeed, transfer, ON or OFF

7. compare the fuel quantity in the tank with the indication of the electronic fuel quantity system.

8. An underwing or single-point pressure fueling system.

9. reduces fueling time, eliminates aircraft skin damage, and reduces chances of contamination.

10. The tank is pressurized with up to 1/2 psi air pressure and liquid soap is added to detect leaks.

11. An internal component fuel leak (shutoff valve, selector valve, or crossfeed valve).

12. Sight glass, mechanical, electrical, and electronic.

13. It measures by weight instead of volume.

14. resist surging from changes in the attitude of the aircraft

15. allow water and sediment to settle to the drain point.

16. drain the water out of the tanks

CHAPTER 15

FILL IN THE BLANKS

1. airfoils and air inlets
2. moisture, freezing temperatures
3. lighter, of little
4. rime, clear
5. icing, performance, deteriorate
6. thermal, electrical, and chemical anti-icing systems
7. turbine compressor, engine exhaust heat exchangers, combustion heater
8. computers
9. electric thermal
10. weeping wing
11. pneumatic de-icing system, leading edge
12. vacuum, suction
13. engine-driven air pump (vacuum pump), gas turbine compressors
14. electrical boots or chemical de-ice
15. ice, fog
16. resistance wire, conductive coating
17. ice detector sensors

TRUE or FALSE

1. true
2. true
3. true
4. true
5. true
6. false
7. false
8. true
9. false
10. true
11. false
12. true
13. false
14. true
15. true

MULTIPLE CHOICE

1. a
2. c
3. b
4. a

5. d
6. a
7. a
8. d
9. c
10. c

KNOWLEDGE APPLICATION

1. clear and rime ice

2. a) malformation of the airfoil which could decrease the amount of lift; b) additional weight and unequal formation of the ice which could cause un-balancing of the aircraft.

3. surge, vibration, and complete thrust loss

4. wing leading edges; horizontal and vertical stabilizer leading edges; engine cowl leading edges; propellers, propeller spinner; air data probes; flight deck windows; water and waste system lines and drains.

5. heat surfaces with hot air; heat with electrical elements; breaking up ice with inflatable boots; chemical spray.

6. wing , leading edge slats, horizontal and vertical stabilizer , engine, and wind shield anti-ice.

7. to heat both wings equally, keeping the airplane aerodynamically stable in icing conditions.

8. without a forward speed the leading edge can easily overheat if left on, therefore the ground sensing system (weight on wheels) will disable the system.

9. antifreeze solution is pumped from a reservoir through a mesh screen embedded in the leading edges of the wings and stabilizers. Activated by a switch in the cockpit, the liquid flows over the wing and tail surfaces, deicing as it flows.

10. When deice system is energized, the control valves in each nacelle and deflate valve receive power. The deice control valves route pressurized air from the discharge side of the pump to the deicer boots. At 17 psi, pressure switches on the deflate valve will de-energize the deice control valves, and the boots will be deflated and vacuum pressure will hold the boots down against the leading edge surfaces.

11. a new layer of ice may begin to form on the expanded boots and become un-removable.

12. large amounts of hot air can be bled off the compressor, providing a satisfactory source of anti-icing and deicing heat.

13. pumps have carbon vanes and parts that self lubricate.

14. windshield wipers, chemical rain repellent, pneumatic rain removal (jet blast), or the windshields are treated with a hydrophobic surface seal coating.

CHAPTER 16

FILL IN THE BLANKS

1. Colorless, odorless, tasteless
2. Aviator Breathing Oxygen
3. 50, water vapor
4. Demand-flow
5. Diluter-demand, pressure-demand
6. Moisture
7. 8,000 ft, cruising altitude
8. Pressurization, depressurization
9. Supercharger, turbocharger, engine driven compressor
10. Bleed air
11. Isobaric, differential
12. Cabin altitude, rate of change, barometric pressure
13. Outflow valve
14. Electrically, cabin pressure controller
15, Over pressurization
16. Negative relief valves

17. Vapor cycle, air cycle
18. Engine compressor, APU
19. Refrigeration turbine unit, air cycle machine
20. Thermistors, resistance
21. Liquid, vapor
22. Receiver dryer
23. Copper, aluminum
24. Exhaust gases
25. Cleaning filters, spark plug

TRUE or FALSE

1. true
2. false; they are painted green.
3. true
4. false; indicates that the pressure relief valve has opened and this should be investigated.
5. true
6. true
7. false; below 8,000
8. true
9. false; turbochargers are the most common.
10. false; turbochargers are driven by exhaust gases.
11. true
12. false; differential control mode of a cabin pressurization system controls pressure to maintain a constant pressure between the air outside the cabin and the ambient air.
13. true
14. false; prevent cabin over pressurization.
15. true
16. true
17. false; a swirling motion will separate the water droplets.
18. true
19. false; It is an closed system
20. false; R134-A has replaced R12
21. true
22. false. should feel cool.
23. true
24. false; use a exhaust shroud heating system.
25. false; drawn from an aircraft fuel tank.

KNOWLEDGE APPLICATION

1. outflow valve
2. Bleed air from the turbine-engine compressor
3. The cabin pressure controller.
4. Gasoline combustion heater, electric heater, and exhaust shroud heat exchanger.
5. carry the heat where it is needed
6. expansion turbine, air-to-air heat exchangers, water separator, and various temperature control valves.
7. The compressed air turns a turbine, and it undergoes a pressure and temperature drop.
8. moist air passes through a fiberglass bag that condenses the moisture in droplets, vanes swirl the air and droplets are collected and drained.
9. The compressor pressurizes low pressure vapor into high pressure vapor. The condenser cools the high pressure vapor with outside air and turns it into a high pressure liquid. At the expansion valve the high pressure liquid changes into a low pressure liquid. In evaporator the low pressure liquid absorb s cabin heat and change into a low pressure vapor and returns to the receiver dryer where the process is repeated again.
10. When the pack valve opens hot high pressure bleed air flows to air mix valve. Depending on temperature a certain amount of this bleed air travels to the mixing chamber and the rest flows to the primary heat exchanger to be cooled. The bleed air will travel through a second mixing valve and enters the compressor of the air cycle machine. The pressure and temperature of the bleed air increases. The bleed air will flow through the secondary heat exchanger where its temperature is lowered by ambient air. After the secondary heat exchanger the air enters the aircycle machine. Here the air temperature lowers because energy in the air drives the turbine which in turn drives the compressor. The shape of the turbine blades expand the air which lowers in pressure and temperature. The air that leaves the air cycle machine flows through the water separator where moisture is removed. When the sensor at the water separator senses 35 degrees the anti-ice control valve opens to allow warmer air to mix with the air leaving the air cycle machine. The air that leaves the water separator will flow to the mixing chamber where it is mixed with hot bleed air. Temperature control is realized by positioning the two mixing valves so that the desired temperature is achieved.
11. A receiver dryer, evaporator, compressor, condenser, and expansion valve.
12. oxygen flows from a charged cylinder through a high-pressure line to a reducing valve and to mask outlets.
13. system must be purged to remove moisture
14. dry nitrogen, dry air, or oxygen
15. aviators' breathing oxygen
16. provide lubrication and prevent compressor failure
17. use oil free tools, clothing, hands, adequate eye protection
18. turbocharger, supercharger, engine driven compressor
19. small amount of LOX can be converted to an enormous amount of gaseous oxygen, thus needing little storage space.
20. cabin altitude, rate of change, and barometric correction and pressurization mode

CHAPTER 17

FILL IN THE BLANKS

1. a fixed fire protection
2. thermal switch system, thermocouple system, continuous-loop detector system.
3. rate of temperature rise, slowly
4. chromel and constantan
5. thermistor, Lingberg
6. nacelle temperature
7. AND
8. Systron-Donner, Meggitt safety systems
9. lavatories, cargo, smoke
10. flame detectors
11. reciprocating, carbon monoxide, exhaust system
12. water, ignition
13. Carbon dioxide
14. high Rate of Discharge (HRD), 1 to 2
15. liquid, gas

TRUE or FALSE

1. true
2. false
3. false
4. false
5. true
6. false
7. true
8. true
9. false
10. true

MULTIPLE CHOICE

1. 3
2. 2
3. 1
4. 2
5. 4
6. 1
7. 4
8. 4
9. 2
10. 3

KNOWLEDGE APPLICATION

1. Engines and APU, Cargo and baggage compartments, Lavatories, Electronic bays, Wheel wells, Bleed air ducts.
2. Overheat detectors, Rate-of-temperature-rise detectors, Flame detectors, Observation by crewmembers.
3. Rate-of-temperature-rise detectors, Radiation sensing detectors, Smoke detectors, Overheat detectors, CO2 detectors, Combustible mixture detectors, Optical detectors.
4. Fenwal, Kidde, and Lingberg
5. Precise fit, eliminates chafing, and quick and easy to install.
6. Fire detection and extinguishing for engines, APUs, cargo bays, and bleed air systems.
7. Halocarbon Clean Agents, Halon, and dry powders.
8. Turbine engines, APU, Cargo compartments, lavatories
9. cartridge (squib) and frangible disc type valve
10. to rupture the frangible disk
11. This is an indication for the maintenance crew that the fire extinguishing system was activated by the flight crew.
12. The engine will stop because the fuel control shuts off, the engine will be isolated from the aircraft systems, and the fire extinguishing system will be activated.
13. The presence of a fire would be easily discovered by a crewmember while at his station; and each part of the compartment is easily accessible in flight.
14. Class B has a smoke detector or fire detection system.
15. The master warning lights come on, the fire warning aural operates, a cargo fire warning message shows, the cargo fire warning light comes on.
16. Kinks and sharp bends can cause an internal wire to short intermittently to the outer tubing and cause false alarms.
17. 550 psi